HELPING CHURCH TEENS DEAL

SEX

WITH CHALLENGING ISSUES

HELPING CHURCH TEENS DEAL

WITH CHALLENGING ISSUES

Beth Robinson

COVENANT
PUBLISHING

www.covenantpublishing.com

P.O. Box 390 Webb City, Missouri 64870
Call toll free at 877.673.1015

Library of Congress Cataloging-in-Publication Data

Robinson, Beth, 1964-
   Sex: helping church teens deal with challenging issues / Beth Robinson.
      p. cm.
Includes bibliographical references.
   ISBN 1-892435-37-3 (pbk.)
   1. Sex—Religious aspects—Christianity—Study and teaching. 2. Christian education
of teenagers. I. Title.
   BT708.R55 2003
   241'.66—dc21
                              2002156713

Dedication

This book is dedicated to my students
who continue to teach me
about the sexual challenges teens and young adults encounter.

Acknowledgments

Writing this book would have been a difficult task without the support of Christi, Treca, Sarah, and Gerrit. They encouraged me and took care of the daily distractions to help me carve out time to write. Thanks!

I can't explain the influence my mom and dad have had on my writing. From as early as I can remember they both encouraged me to read and write. They've read and reread countless papers and articles. I appreciate the years of encouragement.

The whole concept of this book belongs to Mike Kennedy. He gave me the idea and kept after me to follow through with writing this. He took the book to a publisher and persuaded me to be persistent in trying to get this published. Mike, and his wife, Karen, read and reread the chapters in this book countless times. I appreciate all the support!

I appreciate Steve Cable, John Hunter, and Covenant Publishing for taking a chance on an unknown author. Having a "personal editor" and marketing agent have made this a delightful process. Working with two men who are interested in pursuing God's will in their publishing endeavors is a remarkable experience.

Several readers looked over this manuscript. Insightful comments from Carole Carroll, John Delony, Rudy Muñoz, Latayne Scott, Andy Young, and other readers have strengthened this book considerably!

Most of us feel awkward,
and perhaps even threatened,
when trying to discuss sex with teens.
Few of us experienced having an open
discussion with our own parents about
sexual issues as we were growing up.
The very thought of discussing sex
can cause us to feel anxious.
Yet, we must move from where we are
to where teens are if we are going to
help them develop an awareness of
sexuality and an understanding
of healthy boundaries.

Preface

I've written *Sex: Helping Church Teens Deal with Challenging Issues* to help youth ministers and church youth workers respond to the sexual issues of adolescence and understand the role that sexual issues play in shaping teenagers' identities and spiritual values. During the past sixteen years, I've worked with teens in a variety of roles. I've been a counselor, foster parent, mentor, church volunteer, teacher, coach, and Christian camp volunteer. In the course of working with teens, I've become convinced that, as Christian adults, we must aggressively educate our teens in church groups about sexuality.

We live in a society that sells sex as the cure for loneliness, depression, anxiety, and isolation. Our culture calls teens to engage in lives of promiscuous sexual involvement with multiple partners outside of a marriage relationship. The media inundates our teens with messages endorsing premarital sex, homosexual relationships, involvement in pornography, and sexual harassment and violence.

As a result of cultural norms and media endorsement, our teens are confused about sexual issues. Regrettably, we, as Christians, have been too silent in our response to teens. I am constantly amazed in my discussions with teens at their openness to talking about sexuality and their overwhelming desire for honesty and guidance. When I talk with college students, they frequently recount their experiences with how churches handled sexual issues. Teens tell me:

"We need more than generalities about sexual purity."

"Don't tell us not to do 'it' when we don't even know what 'it' is."

"We know about pregnancies and STDs, but how is that connected with dating?"

"Adults try to scare us into not being involved in sex, but there's nothing scary about the sex we see in movies or on TV."

Although I wish we lived in a culture that promoted Christian perspectives of sexuality, I am forced to accept that our teens will be bombarded with messages contrary to biblical teaching in our culture. While I certainly advocate that adults provide boundaries about where teens go and what they listen to and view on TV, realistically teens are going to encounter numerous messages about sexuality, despite our efforts to shield them from some of the most graphically sexual material. We are forced to respond to what our culture teaches about sexuality or we inadvertently endorse cultural messages about sexuality with our silence.

Although my colleagues consider me a competent professional counselor, I recognize that there are no easy answers to sexual issues, questions, and struggles when working with teens. In writing this book, I focused on issues that I thought youth ministers and youth workers would encounter. The first section of the book, *Getting Your Feet Wet*, is about recognizing how our own personal feelings and beliefs impact how we address sexual issues with teens. The second, *Knowing Where Teens Are*, deals with teen development, dating, setting boundaries, and cultural messages about sex. The third section, *Handling Challenging Issues*, addresses pregnancies, STDs, abortion, sexual harassment, pornography, homosexuality, and sexual violence. The fourth section, *Handling Church Issues*, outlines methods for screening and supervising youth workers to prevent sexual incidents in youth groups.

Although the interventions and strategies discussed in this book reflect my Christian worldview, this book isn't intended to be a theological discussion about sex. Rather it's intended to provide practical strategies to enhance the ability of church youth workers to communicate and connect with teens in a meaningful way concerning sexual issues. In writing this book, I've tried to approach issues and problems in an honest way and to offer viable preventative strategies and interventions.

Whenever possible, I've used case studies to supplement the materials presented in this book. The case studies are based on actual incidents. I've changed some identifying information and details to protect the identities of teens. However when you read the case studies and begin to think that a similar situation would not occur in your youth group, remember that all these incidents have actually occurred in similar youth groups. The case studies are drawn from many different youth groups, not just youth groups where I've worked with teens.

The purpose of this book is to equip youth workers and youth ministers to respond to challenging sexual issues and to help teens understand and implement biblical values for sexuality. It's my hope and prayer that God will use this book as an effective tool for equipping youth workers to help teens deal with sexual issues.

Table of Contents

SECTION THREE: Handling Challenging Issues

SECTION FOUR: Handling Church Issues

SECTION ONE
Getting Your Feet Wet

The *focus* of this section is to help you explore your own personal values about sexual issues.

The *purpose* of this section is to help you clearly understand your own values so that you can be more comfortable in addressing sexual issues with teens. In addition, you are encouraged to explore the Bible and develop a clear understanding of what the Bible teaches about sexuality.

Chapter 1
Get Real!

If we remain silent in discussions
about sexuality, teens will
turn to other sources.
I pray that we will be a loud voice
and a reassuring safe place in a
tumultuous time for young people.
We don't want to abdicate our
responsibility to address sexual
issues to other sources.
We want teens to feel comfortable
discussing their fears, their
concerns, and their mistakes with us.

1
Get Real!

David Gonzales can't wait to become a youth minister. He is convinced that he can provide the spiritual guidance that teens need to negotiate daily challenges in their lives. He attended church camps and was active in youth group growing up. While he was preparing for youth ministry, he spent two summers as an intern in congregations and worked for the last year as an intern with a junior high youth group. He is convinced that teens trust him and value his advice. His first full-time youth ministry job is at a congregation with about 40 teenagers.

David enjoys interacting with teens and encouraging them to live their lives based on Christian values. He likes the challenge of preparing lessons and devotionals that speak to the heart of teens. He even enjoys the chaotic pressure of preparing for retreats and weekly activities. God prepared him for this ministry at this point in time.

Only one issue weighs heavy on his heart. Nothing in his training prepared him to help teens deal with sexual issues. He thinks about the discussions he had during the past two weeks. He talked with six different teens who had concerns about sexual issues:

"My girlfriend wants to have sex, but I think it is wrong. She says I'm scared. She's right—I am!"

"I'm pregnant. I can't tell my parents. Will I go to hell if I get an abortion?"

"I'm gay. Do you think anyone will accept me if they know?"

"I asked my boyfriend to stop, but he didn't. Is that rape?"

"I've got herpes. What do I do? My parents will kick me out of the house if they find out I've been having sex."

"My stepfather visits my bedroom as soon as mom leaves for

work. She loves him. She'll never believe that he is forcing me to have sex with him. What should I do?"

David tries a variety of strategies with these six teens including prayer, Bible study, peer counseling, and pastoral counseling. Sometimes he thinks he makes a difference in helping teens deal with sexual issues, but mostly he wonders what he can do to be more effective. He honestly admits that he is uncomfortable discussing sexual issues with teens. The "sex talk" even triggers some feelings of anxiety for David as he recalls his own sexual experiences during adolescence and how little help his well-meaning parents were. David recognizes that he will have to explore his own values concerning sexuality.

Many of the teens in David's youth group discuss experiences far different from his own. They live lives that he only reads about. His training for youth ministry included little coverage of sexual issues. He worries that he might have to discuss subjects viewed as inappropriate by parents or the church leadership. In fact, when he thinks teens want to discuss sexual issues, he frequently redirects the conversation to other subjects. Yet he knows that counseling adolescents positively about sex is extremely important for their growth.[1]

A Reality Check

Today's teenagers are constantly inundated with messages about sex. They spend four to six hours per day interacting with mass media in various forms. Barna[2] reports that 94% of teens listen to the radio, 89% watch television, 91% listen to audiotapes or compact discs, 69% read a magazine, 52% use the Internet and 58% read a book in a typical day. Although we have come to accept mass media as a part of our daily lives, consider for a moment the messages mass media presents to teenagers about sex.

- Typically, sexual activities occur between two unmarried individuals on television programs or in movies.
- Homosexual characters have become an integral part of movie and television plots.
- Sexuality is mentioned in a casual, and sometimes even a degrading, manner in song lyrics.
- Teen magazines present articles on how to improve one's sex appeal and how to entice a peer into a sexual relationship.

Today's teens may say they are not influenced by mass media, yet how can teens spend four to six hours a day interacting with various forms of mass media and not be influenced by its content? Indeed, teens may report they are not influenced by mass media because they have come to accept its messages. As a result, teens no longer realize how contrary these messages are to biblical teachings.

In addition to being influenced by the media, teens are exposed to an array of messages from their peers. Teens enter a world where sexual promiscuity is an accepted, and even encouraged, behavior. Many young people share the details of their sex lives with friends in intimate details. Sex on the first or second date can easily become the norm for teens concerned about being labeled as prudes. Some teens view sex with multiple partners as part of normal adolescent sexuality.

Of course there are teenagers who are exploring their sexuality and incorporating it into their identity through a Christian worldview. Teens are looking to adults to provide guidance and boundaries as they explore their sexuality. Some teens want to save sex for the marital relationship. These teens seek guidance in youth groups about emulating Christ as they cope with their sexuality.

In the real world, many young people are searching for answers to questions about themselves. Although adolescence is a natural time of sexual exploration and development, changing bodies and unpredictable emotions still confuse teens. In addition to normal adolescent development, increasing numbers of teens are dealing with sexual abuse, sexual harassment, pregnancy, sexually transmitted diseases, and other sexual issues. Effective youth workers cannot avoid addressing sexual concerns. In fact, how they relate to teens and their concerns—sexual or not—will certainly determine their success as youth ministers or youth workers.

What Are My Personal Values?

Generally, the most challenging aspect of working with teens is facing our own personal values and beliefs about sex. Most of us feel awkward, and perhaps even threatened, when trying to discuss sex with teens. Few of us experienced having an open discussion with our own parents about sexual issues as we were growing up. The very thought of discussing sex can cause us to feel anxious. Yet, we must move from where we are to where teens are if we are going to help them develop an awareness of sexuality and an understanding of healthy boundaries.

Frequently, parents and youth workers respond that all we need to do is present the biblical and theological arguments in regards to sex and not discuss the issue any further. Certainly, our teens need to know biblical principles concerning sex. However, in many cases, they may benefit enormously from an open and candid discussion about their personal concerns and issues in regards to sex. While biblical principles are certainly the guidelines we would hope for teens to incorporate in their lives, we must meet them where they are and help them incorporate biblical values into their lives.

If we remain silent in discussions about sexuality, teens will turn to other sources: peers, television, magazines, music, and other worldly influences. I pray that we will be a loud voice and a reassuring safe place in a tumultuous time for young people. We don't want to abdicate our responsibility to address sexual issues to other sources. We want teens to feel comfortable discussing their fears, their concerns, and their mistakes with us.

Having said that, I don't think it is an easy step to move from a desire to help teens address sexual issues to developing the skills and comfort level needed to effectively interact with them about sex. The first step is a willingness to examine our own beliefs, values, and views about sex. One of the most interesting dialogues I have in my college classes with students every semester involves beliefs about sexuality. A typical conversation goes something like this:

"What do you believe about homosexuality?"

"The Bible says it is wrong."

"Since the Bible says it is wrong, would you allow homosexuals to attend your church?"

"That would depend on a lot of things. Are the homosexual people practicing that lifestyle?"

"They aren't currently practicing the lifestyle, and they want to change."

"Then I think they should be welcomed in the church, and the church staff members and leaders should work with them to deal with their homosexuality."

"Okay, what if they are currently sexually involved with someone of the same gender?"

"The church leaders and staff members should study with them to show them that homosexuality is wrong."

"Suppose homosexual people study the Bible and still don't want to change."

"I don't think they should come to church then. They obviously don't believe in the Bible."

At this point in the dialogue, I nod and look a bit puzzled, then I abruptly change the direction of the dialogue.

"What do you think about a person who is married having an affair?"

"The Bible says it is wrong."

"Since the Bible says it is wrong, would you allow a person who is having an extramarital affair to attend your church?"

"Probably, but I think the church leaders and staff members should confront the person about the affair."

"Suppose when the person was confronted, he or she didn't end the affair. What do you think should happen then?"

"The church leaders and staff members need to study with the person who is having an extramarital affair to help him or her see that it is wrong."

"What if even after studying with the church leaders, the person continues to have an affair, what needs to happen then?"

I usually get a wide variety of answers to the second scenario, but the responses are rarely as strong as the responses are to the homosexual scenario. Most students recommend that the church continue to work with a person having an affair, but they recommend that the church cut off interactions with a person who is homosexual. The point of the dialogue is to help students recognize that more than biblical principles affect what we believe about sexual issues. The way we are raised in our families as well as other cultural influences impact our views about sex.

VALUES EXPLORATION WORKSHEET 1
What Do You *Really* Believe?

This worksheet is designed to help you develop a greater awareness of your personal values and views about a variety of sexual issues. The scenarios presented are developed only to help *you* explore *your* own values.

1. You unexpectedly drop by to visit your 19-year-old son who is in college. He has recently moved into an apartment with a new roommate. When you knock on the door, your son's roommate answers the door. She is scantily clad and you see a partially clothed male on the couch. You introduce yourself, and she indicates your son is not in the apartment at that time.
• What about this situation would bother you?

_____

_____

- What would you expect your son to do?

  _____

- Would it change your response if your son assures you that his roommate was in a committed, monogamous relationship?

  _____

- Would it change your response if your son's roommate is male rather than female?

  _____

- Would it change your response if your son's roommate is female and involved in a lesbian relationship?

  _____

  _____

2. You generally eat lunch at work, but one day you run home at lunch to pick up some paper work for the office. When you get home, your sixteen-year-old daughter's car is parked in the driveway and the door is unlocked. You walk into the house and call out to your daughter, but she doesn't immediately respond. You walk back to her room and the door is shut. You knock and open the door. Your daughter and her boyfriend are lying on the bed with their arms wrapped around each other. Your daughter's shirt is unbuttoned, but her boyfriend is fully clothed.

- How would you respond to this situation?

  _____

- What would you expect your daughter to do?

  _____

- Would you react differently if your daughter were 13 years old?

  _____

- Would you react differently if your daughter were 19 years old?

  _____

  _____

3. One of the most active males in your youth group asks to talk with you after a devotional. He is obviously uncomfortable and moves restlessly from foot to foot. He looks down at the floor, and blurts out, "I think I'm gay." He hurriedly looks up to watch your reaction to him.

- What would you say to this teen?

  _____

  _____

- How would this disclosure change your feelings toward him?

- Would you have any idea about how to help?

4. Your 15-year-old sister seems distant and withdrawn. She rarely attends youth group activities or participates in other social activities with her peers. Until the last two or three months, she has always been outgoing and actively involved in peer activities. When you confront her about how she is isolating herself, she begins to cry. She tells you that she is not comfortable attending youth activities. As you ask more questions, your sister tells you that one of the college students who works with the youth group offered to give her a ride home from a youth activity three months ago. Instead of driving her home, he drove her to an unfamiliar part of town and forced her to have sex with him. She has not told anyone else about this incident.

- What would you say to your sister?

- How would this disclosure change how you feel toward your sister?

- How would this disclosure change how you feel toward the college student?

- Would you have any idea how to help your sister cope with this situation?

5. You are expecting houseguests and have asked your son to clean his room. The houseguests will be staying in his room, so you check the room to make sure it is appropriately prepared for them. One of his dresser drawers is ajar. You pull the drawer open and find clothes in total disarray. Silently you berate your son for his messiness and decide to refold the clothes in the drawer. As you begin sorting through the clothes, you are stunned to find several pornographic magazines hidden under the clothing.

- How would you respond to this situation?

- What would you expect your son to do?

- How would this change your interactions with your son?

  _____

  _____

- Would you react differently if you found pornographic material in your daughter's room?

  _____

  _____

Hopefully, the previous exercise helped you recognize how our reactions to sexuality and sexual situations are based on more than biblical knowledge. Some of the previous situations may have caused you discomfort. What made you uncomfortable? Where did you learn this discomfort? Can you deal with your own discomfort and effectively interact with teens when discussing their sexuality? Will your discomfort be a barrier to working with teens?

You may have dismissed some of the situations as unrealistic or unlikely to happen. Let me assure you, I've dealt with similar situations in working with church youth. Teens may not feel comfortable discussing these situations with their parents or their youth ministers; but their discomfort isn't in any way an indicator that they don't face these situations or similar situations. The only question is whether our church teens will face these challenges alone or with the guidance, comfort, and support of knowledgeable adults.

What Are My Spiritual Values?

Recognizing how our own experiences and cultural values impact our views of sexuality is certainly a fine place to start, but it isn't enough exploration to help us effectively work with teen sexual issues. The foundation of being able to provide guidance for youths faced with sexual changes and challenges is being confident and clear in our own understanding of the spiritual values that guide sexual relationships. Many of us have been raised with basically one idea about sex—"Don't do it until you are married." Somehow that one idea was supposed to guide us through our own adolescence and enable us to guide other individuals through their teen years. While I agree that waiting until we are married to develop sexual intimacy with another person is what God intended for us all, I would encourage each of you to examine your spiritual beliefs about sexuality in greater depth. While this book is not intended to be a theological discussion about sexuality, we all need to understand the theological foundations providing the basis for our values.

VALUES EXPLORATION WORKSHEET 2
What Does the Bible *Really* Say?

The following questions are provided to help you develop a better understanding of the spiritual foundations for your beliefs about sex. Grab a pen, a Bible, a concordance, and anything else that will help you answer these questions.

1. What does the Bible teach about sex in the context of a marriage relationship?

_____

_____

_____

2. What guidelines does the Bible provide for helping teens set physical and sexual boundaries when they are dating?

_____

_____

_____

3. What does the Bible teach about masturbation?

_____

_____

_____

4. What does the Bible teach about abortion?

_____

_____

_____

5. What does the Bible teach about sex outside of marriage?

_____

_____

_____

6. What does the Bible teach about homosexuality?

_____

_____

_____

7. What does the Bible teach about rape or incest?

_____

_____

_____

8. What does the Bible teach about pornography?

_____

_____

_____

9. How does our understanding of God's plan for sex impact how we deal with teens in our youth groups?

_____

_____

_____

These questions aren't comprehensive, but they provide a foundation for exploring our values about sex. In grappling with these questions, we can develop a better understanding of God's plan for sexuality. Once we firmly understand our own values about sex, we can begin to develop the skills necessary to effectively provide guidance and assistance to teens facing sexual confusion or challenges.

Warning: Integrity Required

While clearly understanding what we believe about sexual issues is important in working with teens, it's not enough. We must constantly hold ourselves accountable to biblical standards. If we're going to help teens deal with sexual issues, we must have the personal integrity to model those beliefs for our teens. If we're involved in inappropriate sexual relationships or behaviors, we don't need to be working with teens. We need to get our own lives in order before we try to help others.

A youth worker who is watching pornography or is engaged in a premarital sexual relationship cannot provide the spiritual guidance for teens struggling with sexual issues. Youth workers must have a clear idea of biblical teachings concerning sexuality and must be willing to communicate these principles to young people. Youth workers who are unsure about what the Bible teaches or who are hesitant to communicate these beliefs to teens will not be effective. Teens get lots of ambiguous messages about sexual boundaries every day. What teens need from youth workers are clear messages about sexual boundaries and appropriate dating relationships.

The Challenge

Dealing with teen sexuality is not a task for the faint of heart. Facing our discomfort about sex requires courage. Examining our spiritual values demands serious study, contemplation, and prayer. Daring to reach out and help teens as they struggle with sexual issues requires commitment.

As daunting as this task may seem, abdicating the responsibility to others is more frightening. If we can't or won't help teens understand their sexuality, there are others who will provide teens with guidance. The movies they watch, the music they listen to, and the magazines they read all provide messages about sex. If we are silent, who will counter the messages that are contrary to God's teaching? Sexually active peers are willing to teach our teens about sex. If we are silent, who will encourage our teens to remain pure and save themselves for their marriage partners?

If we are silent, our teens may never understand God's wonderful plan for sex.

Can we afford to remain silent?

RESPONDING TO THE CHALLENGE

1. The lessons we learned about sexuality when we were teens can influence how we view sexual issues as an adult. What lessons did you learn about sexuality as a teen that still influence you today?

_____

_____

_____

2. Certain sexual issues may be difficult for you to discuss with teens. Which sexual issues are going to be the most difficult for you in working with teens?

_____

_____

_____

3. If you have previously engaged in sexual behaviors outside a marriage relationship, what have you done to address these behaviors? Are your boundaries strong enough to help a teen with a similar issue?

_____

_____

_____

The foundation of being able to
provide guidance for youths faced with
sexual changes and challenges is
being confident and clear in our
own understanding of the spiritual
values that guide sexual relationships.
If we're going to help teens deal
with sexual issues, we must have
the personal integrity to model
those beliefs for our teens.

SECTION TWO
Knowing Where Teens Are

The *focus* of this section is to help you understand teen culture and adolescent development and how they impact the way teens handle sexual issues. In addition, healthy dating relationships and setting physical and sexual boundaries are explored.

The *purpose* of this section is to help you equip teens to handle cultural pressures about sexuality so they can make good decisions about dating and sexual boundaries.

Teens get lots of ambiguous messages
about sexual boundaries every day.
What teens need from youth workers
are clear messages about
sexual boundaries and appropriate
dating relationships.
Dealing with teen sexuality is
not a task for the faint of heart.
Facing our discomfort about
sex requires courage.
Examining our spiritual values
demands serious study,
contemplation, and prayer.
Daring to reach out and
help teens as they struggle with
sexual issues requires commitment.

2.

I'm Okay. What's Wrong with You?

The first night Janet volunteers to help with teens at church, she is overwhelmed by the energy and chaos created by a group of teens. She feels out-of-place and out-of-touch. They chatter and scatter aimlessly around the room. As she circulates around the groups in the room, she quickly notices how much of the conversation in the groups focused on dating or discussing someone of the opposite sex. Although Janet is almost thirty and has a husband and kids, the anxiety and curiosity of these teens about dating and sexuality triggers memories of her own adolescence.

People who know Janet as an adult see a competent woman who seems to effortlessly juggle the demands of marriage, parenting, and career. She seems at ease with her self and her life. Yet as she remembers adolescence, she suddenly feels awkward and anxious again. She remembers … how much she dreaded her periods … how she worried that her breasts were never going to develop … how awkward she felt about her first kiss … and how scary all the changes in her body were to her. Despite the passage of time, she relives the painful naïveté of an adolescent struggling to integrate her sexuality into her identity. Janet knows she would never want to subject herself again to the anxiety she felt as a teen about her own sexuality and sexual development. She wonders if she can work with the teens at her church.

Getting into the Mind of a Teen

Despite Janet's initial concerns about her skills, her ability to remember how awkward she felt about her own sexuality during adolescence will help her respond more sensitively to the concerns of the teens in the youth group. As we get older and move further away from our adolescent experiences, it is easy to forget how anxious and overwhelmed we felt about sexual issues as a teen. Remembering our own insecurities and awkwardness about sex can prevent us from minimizing the concerns teens have about sexual issues.

Teenagers still experience those feelings of uncertainty and awkwardness. The only difference today is that they must make decisions about sexuality at younger ages. Most adolescent girls begin dating by age 12 or 13, while most boys begin dating by age 13 or 14.[1] By their senior year in high school, most teens date two or three times a month. Once teens begin dating, they begin making decisions about sex. Approximately two-thirds of thirteen-year-old boys and girls have kissed someone. By age sixteen, the majority of girls and boys have engaged in mutual touching and stroking above the waist. By age eighteen, approximately two-thirds of both boys and girls have reported mutual touching and stroking of genital areas below the waist.[2] Approximately one-third of teens experience sexual intercourse by the ninth grade, while slightly more than two-thirds of teens have experienced sexual intercourse by the time they are seniors in high school.[3] Although teens are making decisions about engaging in sexual activity at younger ages, they frequently have only limited knowledge about their own sexuality.

In working with church teens, we must understand adolescent development to be effective in helping teens deal with their developing sexuality. Without an understanding of adolescent development, we may misunderstand the behavior of teens. Teens are experiencing changes physically, emotionally, and intellectually. If we don't understand these changes, we'll view teens as being difficult and arrogant. Because of how teens think, they do genuinely seem to believe at times that they are okay, and the adults are the ones with a problem. When we see teens engaging in high-risk behaviors and ignoring the consequences, we try to warn them. In response, they view us as being the ones with the problem. Quite literally, a teen believes, "I'm okay. What's wrong with you?"

If we are to work effectively with teens, we have to understand the fundamental concepts that adolescence begins in biology and ends in culture. Literally, the marker of the beginning of adolescence is the onset of puberty. Puberty is occurring earlier for both males and females. Many females are beginning to menstruate when they are 11. As a result, adolescence is beginning earlier than it did thirty years ago when girls typically began to menstruate at age 13.[4]

As adolescence is beginning at a younger age, it is also extending for more years. The markers of the end of adolescence are financial, emotional, and social independence. Adolescents obtain adult status when they financially support themselves, develop their own emotional support system, and establish their own families. While legally, adolescents are granted all adult privileges between the ages of 18 and 21, the reality is many adolescents aren't independent from their parents until they are 25 to 30 years old. Adolescence is extending because more youths are pursuing college degrees, graduate degrees, and delaying marriage until their mid-twenties. The average age of marriage for women is 25 and for men is 26.[5]

Adolescence used to be conceived as lasting from ages 13 to 18. Today a more realistic concept is adolescence extending from age 11 until 25 years of age or older. If adolescence is conceptualized as lasting for approximately 15 years, then obviously there are significant differences in the stages of adolescence. Adolescence can be conceptualized as having three stages: early adolescence, middle adolescence, and late adolescence. Early adolescence includes "teens" between the ages of 11 and 13. Middle adolescence extends from ages 14 to 17, and later adolescence extends from 18 years until independence is obtained.

Early Adolescence. During early adolescence, from ages eleven to thirteen, teens make their first attempts to leave the secure role of a child and to establish themselves as independent from their parents. As a result, they begin to realize their parents aren't perfect and focus on parental faults. During early adolescence, teens experience rapid physical growth and change. In addition, in early adolescence, teens are beginning to develop a sense of personal identity. As a result, they frequently want to conform to their peers. The worst possible scenario for a teen in early adolescence is to be seen by peers as being "different." In early adolescence, teens tend to be intensely moody and emotional. In regards to sexuality, they tend to be modest and shy about sexual issues and have concerns about whether their own development is normal. They may also begin to experiment with sex, drugs, cigarettes, and alcohol.

Middle Adolescence. From ages fourteen to seventeen, teens begin to develop new thinking skills and begin to see the world from different perspectives than their own. They continue to establish psychological independence from their parents and begin preparing for adult roles. While peers are still important to teens in this stage, teens in middle adolescence are increasingly self-directed and not as reliant on conforming to peer expectations. By middle adolescence, teens are beginning to control some of their impulsiveness and begin to be concerned about doing what is right. Their concern with doing right may lead to anxiety and guilt about their intense interest in the opposite sex. During this stage, teens are increasingly interested in how peers of the opposite sex respond to them and are concerned about their sexual attractiveness. They may develop fears that they are homosexual.

Late Adolescence. Adolescents between the ages of eighteen and approximately twenty-five begin their final preparation for adult roles. They try to develop vocational goals and begin to have a clear sense of personal identity. The need for peer approval decreases substantially. In late adolescence, teens have typically become psychologically independent from their parents. However, some of the developmental tasks of late adolescence may extend into young adulthood. They are generally concerned with developing serious relationships with the opposite sex and have a clearer sense of sexual identity. In addition, they generally have made a moral decision concerning their willingness to engage in sexual activities outside a marriage relationship.

Obviously, adolescents need spiritual guidance in dealing with sexual issues at all three stages. Yet historically, youth ministry programs have focused on 13 to 18 year olds. Continuing to limit the focus of ministry programs for teens from 13 to 18 year olds overlooks changes in social and emotional development of young people. In recent years, youth ministry programs have begun to extend services down to 11 and 12 year olds. In dealing with sexual issues, it is important to recognize that educational efforts need to occur before teens face situations rather than relying on reactive interventions after teens are involved in sexual situations.

Teens repeatedly tell me that parents, churches, and schools are irrelevant in helping them deal with sexual issues because they have already made decisions about sexual situations before the adults begin to discuss sex with them. If puberty is starting at age 11, then we need to begin discussions in our youth ministry programs before age 11. If children's ministry is still working with youth at age 11, then efforts need to be coordinated with the children's ministry to address sexual situations. Similarly, youth ministers need to work to coordinate services with college and young adult ministries as teens graduate from high school.

In each of the stages of adolescence, teens face challenges in five areas: physical development, emotional development, social development, intellectual development, and spiritual development. Teens don't necessarily deal with each of these issues at exactly the same time, but all teens deal with these developmental issues at some point in their adolescence. Resolving developmental issues in all five areas will help teens move into adulthood with the skills necessary for forming healthy marital relationships and for maintaining a faithful commitment to God.

What's Happening to Me?

Every time you teach class, Josh sits hunkered down on the back row with his hands in his jacket. He doesn't interrupt or try to distract other students, but he refuses to participate in any class activities. One Sunday, you divide the teens into two different groups to play a Bible trivia game. Josh continues to sit hunkered down on the back row with his jacket pulled around him. You're determined to get Josh involved in Bible trivia, but when you push him to join the activity, he walks out of the class.

For the rest of the Bible class, you force yourself to focus on the Bible trivia game, but the whole time you struggle with frustration and anger about Josh. You're angry because he continues to defy you in class and you are frustrated about your inability to connect with him. After the class is over, Josh catches you outside of the classroom.

"Can I talk to you for a minute?"

"Sure, Josh."

"I'm sorry about not playing that game, but ..." his voice trails off.

"Josh, I'm sorry I made such a big deal out of it. I'm just frustrated because you used to be involved in class discussions, but now you seem to dread being here."

"That's not it. I like Bible class, but ... I ... um ... I get embarrassed," responds Josh. Josh's face begins to turn a dark shade of red and he keeps his eyes focused on the floor.

You have no clue what is embarrassing Josh.

"I don't understand Josh. What's embarrassing you?"

"Well ... um ... it's just that lately things happen sometimes. I mean I can't control things and ... Well," Josh hesitates for a moment and takes a deep breath then blurts out, "I get hard ons and it's embarrassing. I don't want everyone to see."

This scenario with Josh points out how teens struggle to cope with the changes in their bodies, particularly in early adolescence. From ages 11 to 14, teens are experiencing rapid change in height and weight. Primary and secondary sexual characteristics are emerging. Females are developing breasts, starting their menstrual cycles, and experiencing rapid mood changes. Males are having wet dreams, growing body hair, and experiencing erections at unwanted times. These changes continue through middle adolescence, but they are not as rapid.

As teens' bodies begin to change, they feel overwhelmed and a bit frightened by their bodies' responses when they are attracted to someone. They feel awkward and embarrassed because they don't understand how their bodies are changing. Rather suddenly, adolescents look less like children and more like physically and sexually mature adults.

With all the physical changes that occur, teens may compare their physical development to that of their peers. Obviously, some teens develop more rapidly than other teens. Teens who develop earlier or later than their friends may feel stressed and embarrassed by their sexual development. If a female develops earlier than other females, she wonders what is wrong with her. If a male is slower developing than other males, he is concerned that he isn't masculine. Teens may interpret early or late development as being weird or disgusting.

In addition to the emotional reactions teens have about their bodies developing earlier or later than their peers, there are some legitimate consequences to being a late or early developing teen. Early maturing males tend to be more self-assured and more popular with their peers during adolescence. Late maturing males tend to be anxious during adolescence and lack self-confidence, but as they move into adulthood, they become more self-assertive and tolerant.[6] Early maturing females tend to have more positive body image, greater peer prestige, and adult approval in adolescence[7]; however, they tend to date sooner and are more often in trouble at school, and at greater risk for engaging in early sex.[8] Late maturing females usually have the advantage of growing taller and thinner than early maturing girls.[9]

Everyone Is Watching

One Wednesday evening after Bible study, Meagan's parents catch you in the hall and ask to speak with you. They describe how Meagan has become obsessed with her appearance. Meagan gets up three hours before school starts to get dressed for the day. She is spending over an hour fixing her hair. When she has a pimple, she refuses to go to school.

Except for completing her homework, the only thing she does is look through fashion magazines. She spends hours looking at "perfect" models. She examines the airbrushed images of models in magazines and doesn't recognize that the images found in magazines are unattainable. Meagan spends every evening planning her clothes, hair, and makeup for the next day. Her parents are concerned about her obsession with her appearance.

Meagan is demonstrating the developmental challenge of being ego-centric. She believes that everyone is watching her and that everyone pays attention to everything she does. Because Meagan believes everyone is watching her and critiquing how she dresses and what she does, she is spending endless hours preparing her appearance. Meagan, like other teens, feels a tremendous pressure to look "perfect." Frequently teens define "perfection" as models depicted in the media. The media models can create an unrealistic expectation and an unattainable standard for appearance. Because teens feel that everyone is watching them, they experience tremendous anxiety about normal development and social situations. They perceive that other people will be scrutinizing their interactions with peers and their sexual development.

Consequences Don't Apply

Amanda was 14 years old when she attended a church youth group activity on a Saturday afternoon. At that youth activity, she met Randy for the first time. After talking for a few minutes, Randy asked her to go out to his car to talk with him. She agreed. Initially they talked in the car, but eventually they started to make out.

They had sex and then returned to the youth group meeting a little later. Several weeks later, Amanda told her youth minister about having sex with Randy. Amanda was stunned at the youth minister's reaction. She had expected a lecture on waiting until she was married to have sex. Instead the youth minister focused on how dangerous it was for her to get in a car with someone she didn't know. Amanda had never considered the danger of the situation. All she had been concerned about was whether Randy would like her or not.

Amanda's experience demonstrates how teens frequently engage in behaviors placing them at physical, social, or emotional risk. Risk taking is a normal part of adolescent development. Teens take risks because of a personal fable. The personal fable is the belief teenagers have that normal consequences do not apply to their actions.[10]

When educational programs aimed at curbing sexual activity are ineffective, it's because teens don't believe that the consequences being discussed in activities will happen to them. Quite literally, teens believe they are immune to the consequences of their actions. Interestingly, they are quite unaware that they have this belief system. Therefore, trying to "teach" them about the consequences of sexual activities can be an extremely frustrating experience for adults.

Teens' idea that they are immune from consequences is most prevalent during early and middle adolescence. Thankfully, teens eventually outgrow the idea that natural consequences do not apply to them. Gradually, teens develop more self-control and begin to evaluate which behaviors are acceptable and mature.

No Previous Experience Required

Imagine that an attractive teen asks to talk with you after a teen devotional. She sits and fidgets in her chair as she twirls her hair in her hand. Finally she glances up at you and says, "I think there is something wrong with me."

You are puzzled because this student doesn't have problems at home or in the youth group.

"Tell me what you mean."

"Something's wrong with me. I've been dating Abdul for a couple of weeks and I'm getting sick all the time."

Immediately, you wonder if this teen is pregnant and is experiencing morning sickness.

"When are you getting sick?"

"Just when we go out."

Mentally, you cross pregnancy off the list of possibilities and consider anxiety as an option.

"Are you nervous about dating Abdul?"

"I was the first time we went out, but I like him a lot and we have a lot of fun."

"Tell me a little more about what happens when you get sick."

"Well, I don't actually throw up, but I feel like I'm going to be sick. I know something awful is wrong with me." The student hesitates for a minute. She looks down at the floor and lets her hair fall to cover her face, "It's just that … hmm … every time Abdul kisses me, my stomach feels sick. I know it's weird. Nobody else gets sick when they kiss guys. What's wrong with me?"[11]

There is nothing "wrong" with this teen, she just doesn't understand what is happening in her body when she is sexually aroused. She is interpreting sexual arousal as being nausea because she doesn't have any previous sexual experience. As teens develop sexually, everything is a new experience: first wet dream, first kiss, first party, first love. The novelty of all these experiences contributes to the intensity of teen responses because they can't compare their current feelings and experiences with any other experiences. Teens anticipate dating, but often experience anxiety when they are asked out on a date because they don't know what is expected in dating situations.

Teens experience lots of different changes in their bodies, changes in their peer groups, changes in their expectations, and changes in what adults expect from them. Each of these areas of change creates anxiety for the teen because they are first-time experiences. Just like learning to drive, they have to learn how to negotiate and manage new expectations and challenges. Eventually, their bodies quit changing and they become comfortable with who they are, but initially, most don't have the necessary skills for handling puberty.

Who Am I Today?

On Tuesday evenings, you invite teens to your home for a Bible study. During the previous two Bible studies, you've noticed that Valerie has been wearing provocative clothing. You are a little astonished at her choices. You've known her family for several years. You can't imagine that her parents are allowing her to wear tight, revealing clothing, especially to a youth group activity. Tonight when she arrives for the Bible study, she is dressed in a shirt with a plunging neckline and a short, skin-tight skirt. Her clothes leave nothing to the imagination.

You realize that for the past six months, Valerie's appearance has changed drastically several times. She used to wear conservative clothes, but seems to be experimenting with several different styles of clothing. When you talk with Valerie and express your surprise at her appearance, she begs you not to tell her parents. She reveals that she has been leaving her parents' house dressed modestly, but then has been stopping and changing her clothes at a friend's house.

Valerie's experimentation with clothing is indicative of how teens explore identity issues. While teens don't consciously decide who they want to be every day, identity exploration and formation is one of the most important developmental tasks of adolescence. Prior to adolescence, a child's identity is generally an extension of their parents' identities. Teenagers begin to recognize their own uniqueness. As a result of recognizing they are not an extension of their parents' identities, teens begin to separate from their parents and develop their own personal identities.

They begin to search for who they are and how they can fit in with their peers. They frequently change clothing, hairstyles, and even types of friends as they try to decide who they want to be. In addition, they may want to announce who they are by wearing strikingly different clothing or by having a tattoo displayed that represents part of their identity.

Part of identity exploration and formation involves teens integrating sexuality into their self-concept. In clarifying what they believe, teens set a foundation for making healthy and responsible decisions about their own sexuality. However, teens may intentionally make choices that clash with their family's spiritual values as a way of distinguishing their own personal identity. A teen raised in a conservative religious home with parents who oppose abortion may participate in a pro-choice organization. Similarly, a teen whose parents have actively voiced the belief that abstinence should be advocated in schools rather than birth control may write an editorial for the school paper advocating the distribution of condoms in schools. These "rebellions" are part of the developmental process of establishing a clear personal identity and are generally transient.

The Challenge

While the material in this chapter may initially seem daunting, you will find that eventually the developmental issues of adolescence will become welcome signposts as you work with teens. If you spend some time reviewing the material in this chapter regularly, you will begin to recognize how these developmental tasks affect the way adolescents interact with you. Teens interact differently in early adolescence than they do in late adolescence and vice versa.

Of all the material presented in the book, this chapter may be the chapter that seems the least connected to how you work with youth in your church, but it is the foundation for how you act and interact when working with teens. You can waste countless hours and tons of energy pursuing strategies that are not developmentally appropriate for teens. If you utilize strategies that are not developmentally appropriate for teens, you may not teach what you want to teach. In fact, you may teach some concepts you really don't want to teach.

If we want to make a difference in the lives of teens, we must meet them where they are. We cannot meet them where they are if we do not understand the developmental issues of adolescence.

RESPONDING TO THE CHALLENGE

1. Based on the information in this chapter, what do you think will be the most challenging tasks in addressing sexual issues with teens in early adolescence? Middle adolescence? Late adolescence?

_____

_____

_____

_____

2. If teens are becoming sexually active at earlier ages, what do youth ministry programs need to do to effectively address sexual issues?

_____

_____

_____

_____

3. As we develop intervention strategies in youth groups for sexual issues, what adolescent developmental concepts do we need to incorporate in our strategies?

_____

_____

_____

_____

As we get older and move further
away from our adolescent experiences,
it is easy to forget how anxious
and overwhelmed we felt about
sexual issues as a teen.
Remembering our own insecurities
and awkwardness about sex
can prevent us from minimizing
the concerns teens have
about sexual issues.

3

You Want Me to Talk about S-E-X?

Every fall Bob teaches a lesson on purity in his youth group class. He stresses the importance of not having sex until marriage and reads Bible verses condemning sexual impurity. He tells a story or two about teens who have become sexually active and gotten pregnant. He emphasizes how this shattered the dreams these teens had for their futures. He generally teaches a long lesson, so there isn't time for discussion or questions from the teens. He isn't comfortable discussing specific information about sex.

The Sunday after he teaches a lesson on purity, he has one of the young married couples in his church come and talk to his youth group about how much it meant to them that their marital partner hadn't been sexually active prior to marriage. Generally, the couple would talk about how important it is not to get in situations where there is the temptation to engage in sexual activities. Again, the presentation is general and presents principles, but not specific information.

On the third Sunday, Bob has a nurse come talk to his youth group about STDs and pregnancy. The nurse shows slides of STDs and talks about the risks of AIDS and death from being sexually active. The nurse also talks about the health risks of being pregnant at an early age and the demands of caring for an infant.

Bob is deliberate in his efforts to deal with sexual issues and schedules this three-part series every year. He changes the presenters and some of the material every year so that it will be more appealing to the teens. Despite these efforts, teens in his youth group continue to be sexually active and deal with issues of pornography, pregnancy, and even homosexuality. Bob is frustrated because he feels ineffective in his efforts to reach teens.

Certainly, Bob is well intentioned, but he is not talking about sex in a way that reaches teens.

I'm Not Comfortable Conversing about Sex

Bob, like many of us, is not comfortable having conversations with teens about sex. Most of us are more comfortable talking around sexual issues, rather than having a conversation about sexual issues. What we must realize is the media is directly promoting sexual promiscuity. If we are going to be effective in teaching our teens about a Godly perspective of sexuality, we have to be just as direct in promoting sexual purity and abstinence.

In writing this book, I wish there were two or three activities I could outline for the reader to be able to complete and then magically be more comfortable having conversations with teens about sexuality. I don't think those two or three magical activities exist. I think for us to be comfortable talking about sex with teens, we have to be willing to talk about sex with our spouses, our kids, and fellow youth ministry workers. Before we are going to be able to have conversations about sex with anyone, we need to recognize the barriers we face in discussing sex.

Barriers to Dialoguing about Sex

- We aren't comfortable talking about sex. We don't talk about sex with our spouses, children, or friends.
- We don't have any role models about how to talk with teens about sex, because no adults talked to us about sex. If someone did talk to us about sex, he or she was generally uncomfortable and embarrassed during the discussion. Very few of us of had role models who were able to comfortably discuss sexual issues with us.
- Many of us grew up in homes and churches where sex was discussed in terms of purity or marital fidelity. Although this may have been effective for previous generations, it is unlikely that it will be as effective today because teens are being inundated daily with sexual information.
- Many of us don't have good sexual knowledge ourselves. We are struggling with sex in our own lives and aren't communicating with the people closest to us about it.
- To effectively discuss sexual issues, we have to be able to have an emotionally intimate conversation. Many of us are not equipped to talk about sex as an emotionally intimate issue.
- We've been told that sex is embarrassing and lewd outside of marriage. We haven't been taught that God created sex to enhance intimacy and communication in marriage.

Until we address and resolve our discomfort with these barriers, we aren't going to be effective in discussing sex with teens. They understand and recognize the barriers even when we don't see them ourselves. The best way to work through these barriers is by having some frank and open discussions with our spouses, friends, and fellow youth workers. Maybe some youth workers aren't able to address sexual issues with teens, but our youth ministry programs are crying out for staff members and volunteers who are equipped to have candid discussions with teens about sex.

Myth versus Reality

In addition to our personal discomfort in discussing sex, there are some misperceptions that influence how we discuss sex in youth ministry programs. These misperceptions allow us the luxury of talking around sexual issues rather than addressing sexual issues directly.

Myth	Reality
Talking about specific sexual information will encourage teens to become sexually active.	If we don't talk about specific sexual information, all the information teens have will be from the media, peers, and the Internet.
Talking about specific sexual information is impure.	God created us in his image and as sexual beings. Sex is part of his plan in creation.
Talking about specific sexual information will only encourage adolescents to be lewd, silly, and vulgar.	If we are comfortable and relevant in talking about sex, teens will be interested and respectful in their interactions.
Teaching teenagers to wait until marriage or just "Say no" is enough sex education.	In teaching teens to wait until marriage, we have inadvertently taught them that anything is acceptable except vaginal intercourse.
Talking about purity is talking about sex.	Talking about purity is too general for teens inundated with specific sexual messages every day. We have to define purity for them in sexual terms.
Talking about STDs and pregnancy is talking about sex.	STDs and pregnancies are consequences of sex. If we don't talk about sex itself, discussions of STDs and pregnancies aren't meaningful to teens.

Teens tell me again and again that what we are saying when we talk about sex isn't connecting with what's going on in their world. Sex is a hush-hush, taboo subject in many churches.

"So in the ninth grade when a girl is felt up for the first time, and it actually feels good and there is seemingly nothing dirty about it, that situation will do nothing but encourage similar behavior in the future. When a guy stumbles on masturbation for the first time, and it has never been discussed or mentioned, save locker room jokes, it turns into a seemingly rewarding behavior with zero consequences. By acting like sex is only to be mentioned by married couples, or by leaving intimate bedroom details to be figured out by two naive people after the stress of a wedding, the nature and beauty of sex is completely distorted to something that can only be messed up."[1]

Teens need someone to talk with them about what to expect in a sexual relationship in marriage and they yearn for someone to have a frank, honest discussion with them about boundaries in a dating relationship.

Teens want us to use the real words and have real information for them. We need to be able to use relatively current terms that are non-medical and non-vulgar terms for genitalia and sexual activities. Teens are hearing terms that refer to orgasms, masturbation, oral sex, anal sex, and erections on television, in school, and from friends. They aren't going to view us as a credible information source if we can't even use sexual terms in a conversation. Only when we are comfortable talking about sexual issues, will we be able to fully use the rest of the information in this chapter.

The Right Thing to Say

Honestly, with teens it is more important that they know you care about them and have their best interest at heart than it is what you say to them. Conversations with teens about sex should emphasize godly principles for guiding sexual and physical contact, while providing encouragement and acceptance for teens. Discussions concerning sex should not become extended conversations where teens recount sexual escapades. Instead, after initially disclosing a sexual issue, the conversations need to be about changing the inappropriate behavior.

Attention Please! Is Anyone Listening? Too often, we are so intent on sharing our wisdom with teens that we don't hear where they are and what is happening in their lives. Listening to teens will strengthen our relationship with them and make it more likely that they will talk to us about sex and other personal issues.

Don't Make Me Say I'm Wrong. Teens need the option of listening to what we say without having to admit we are right. We will get much further in conversations if we don't try to force them to agree with us during the conversation.

Tell It Like It Is! We gain major points for credibility with teens when they know we will be honest and direct in our communication. Teens may not like what we say, but if we are providing factual, truthful information they respect it. Telling it like it is does not mean that we make accusations or value statements. We share factual information.

Tell Me You Understand. Teens feel understood when we reflect their feelings back to them and recognize that feelings are a major aspect of sexual decisions. Acknowledging their emotional responses does not mean that we approve of their behaviors. It simply means we are responsive to their reactions to situations.

Give Me a Safe Place to Talk. Teens feel safe when adults communicate that we are genuinely interested in their lives and are positive in our reactions to what they share with us. In addition, they want to know that we will keep information confidential.

Get It Right. When talking with teens we need to check back with them to make sure we have gotten all the factual information correct and that we have gotten all the relevant information in the situation.

Help Me Find What's Right. Teens are searching for standards defining right and wrong. Often, they are so impacted by media that they don't know what those standards are. Ask teens what they think you would do in that situation. A popular question to ask is "What would Jesus do?" but many teens see this as an unattainable standard. Let them borrow your conscience.

Everybody Else Is Doing It. When teens use this statement to justify their behavior, gently remind them that you are concerned about them, not about everyone else. Reinforce that they are children of God. Talk about their behavior, not everyone else's behavior. If they continue to bring up other people's behavior, remind them that you are talking to them, not everyone else.

Talk about the Tough Stuff. When teens start talking about troubling personal issues, don't avoid the subject. If teens reveal an issue that you don't have the skills to handle, assure teens that you hear what they are telling you and that you will find someone who can help them. Then find someone who can help them.

What Do You Think of Me Now? If teens reveal that they have been engaged in sexual behavior, reassure them that you care about them and emphasize that you still see them as a child of God. Don't condone the behavior, but assure teens that they can change their behavior and find forgiveness in their relationship with God.

Exceptions to Confidentiality

Part of being honest with teens is setting boundaries concerning confidentiality. There are times we cannot keep information confidential because of legal and ethical obligations. Youth workers need to be aware of the laws in their state that impact teens. Although states have different laws, the following situations may require the disclosure of information.

- Most states require that an adult report any suspicions of sexual or physical abuse of a teen.
- If a teen reports to a youth worker that they have engaged in illegal activities, in many states the youth worker may be required to share this information in a police investigation or in court. Illegal activities may include date rape, statutory rape, sexual harassment, and other sexual activities.
- If there is a chance that teens are engaging in high-risk behaviors endangering their safety, youth workers may have to report this behavior to parents or other adults.

In all of these examples, I have used the term "youth worker." Many states protect the confidentiality of information shared with ministers. However, volunteers generally do not have any protection of confidentiality of the information teens share with them.

If I believe teens are going to tell me information that I will have to share with someone else, I tell teens that I may have to share the information with someone else. Surprisingly enough, most teens tell me the information knowing I may have to disclose it to someone. If they tell me information that I need to disclose, I tell them what information I am going to disclose and to whom I am going to tell that information. I also try to prepare them for any consequences that may occur when I disclose information.

Warning: Red Flags

Just as we need to know what to do in talking about sex with teens, we also need to know what not to do. We need to be careful that our conversations are always about encouraging and supporting teens, not about meeting our own sexual needs. Conversations concerning sex with teens shouldn't serve as a turn on for youth workers. Youth workers shouldn't solicit information about the sexual activities of teens as a vicarious sexual experience.

Similarly, if youth workers are struggling with sexual issues themselves, they shouldn't be trying to help teens as a way to work out their own issues. A youth worker who is currently struggling with pornography or homosexuality isn't the person who needs to be ministering to teens struggling with pornography or homosexuality. Certainly youth workers who have overcome struggles with pornography or homosexuality would be excellent role models and mentors for youth struggling with these issues. A good standard is youth workers need to have a minimum of two years without engaging in inappropriate sexual behaviors before they work with youth struggling with sexual issues.

One of the quickest ways to get in trouble as a youth worker is to have extended one-to-one conversations about sexual issues with a teen. Conversations about sexual issues need to involve two adults, even if only one adult does most of the interacting. An adult witness provides some protection against allegations that you are talking about sex inappropriately. Similarly, teens often hear information that is different than what we say. Having an adult witness can help prevent misunderstandings and miscommunication about a sensitive subject.

Conversation Killers

Shoulds and Oughts. Telling teens what they should have done or ought to have done is probably going to completely shut down a conversation. Many times they know what they should have done, but they didn't do it. Now they need help dealing with the consequences of a poor decision.

Not My Problem. Indirectly we communicate to teens that what they are experiencing is not our problem. Frankly, it's not our problem, but if we don't help them with the problem, teens aren't going to make better choices. When we communicate that a situation is not our problem, we leave teens alone in making decisions about their sexuality.

Let Me Tell You About. Jumping in with a story about someone with similar issues is not going to help teens. They don't want to know about other people, they want help with their current situation.

I Can't Believe You Did That. The last thing teens need when they are struggling with sexual issues is for youth workers to criticize their behavior or decisions. Generally teens know they've messed up. They don't need a critique of how badly they messed up.

Here's What You Should Do. Although we may clearly see an effective way to handle a situation, teens don't want someone to tell them what to do. They want youth workers to help them find a way to solve their own problems.

The Challenge

In talking with teens about sex, we need to provide them with confidence that they will be able to deal with their sexual desires in a godly manner. If we can be anchors of hope for teens as they struggle with sexual issues, they have the potential to emerge from adolescence with a healthy view of sex in marriage and healthy boundaries to deal with sexual temptation outside of marriage. If we don't know their struggles and their stories, we can't meet them where they are and help them develop a godly understanding of sexuality.

The challenge for us is to be comfortable having conversations about sex with teens. We have to deal with our own insecurities and anxieties about sex if we are going to provide guidance and mentoring for teens. When we are no longer afraid of talking to teens about sex, we will be effective.

When we are comfortable talking about sex, teens will be comfortable talking to us.

RESPONDING TO THE CHALLENGE

1. Frequently when we are uncomfortable talking about sex, we talk around the subject. What are some ways you have talked around a sexual issue or heard someone else talk around a sexual issue?

_____

_____

_____

_____

2. This chapter outlines some misperceptions of talking about sexual issues. Which of these misperceptions have influenced how you interact with teens?

_____

_____

_____

_____

3. What are the exceptions to confidentiality when talking to teens about sex?

_____

_____

_____

_____

4. What are some red flags indicating youth workers should not be addressing sexual issues with teens?

_____

_____

_____

_____

5. Frequently as adults, we assume the role of a teacher and not a listener. Which of the conversation killers have you struggled with because you are trying to "teach" teens about sex?

_____

_____

_____

_____

Teens need someone to talk
with them about what to expect
in a sexual relationship in marriage
and they yearn for someone to
have a frank, honest discussion
with them about boundaries
in a dating relationship.
Teens want us to use the real
words and have real
information for them.

4

Dating 101: The Real Story

Heather, a beautiful young lady with a group of fun-loving friends, has served as role model for numerous teens. Heather is a single, thirty-year-old, who had a few drinks and had sex with Alex, a male friend. The male friend was wearing a condom, but despite this, Heather gets pregnant.

Heather and Alex are friends, but decide not to marry one another before the baby is born. Heather anticipates being a single mother. However, Alex is going to help in the delivery of their child and wants to be an active parent.

When their daughter is born, Heather's friends are at the hospital to offer their support. One of their friends, Amber, is so excited about the birth of the baby girl that she says, "I'm so glad you guys got drunk and had sex."

Meanwhile two of Heather's friends, Kristin and Barry, are so excited by the birth of the baby that they decide to have a baby of their own. Kristin and Barry, who incidentally are married, decide that the best way to remedy their desire to have a child is by having sex in a janitor's closet.

In the midst of everything that is happening, Alex has decided that he wants to marry Heather and has a ring for her in his pocket when their child is born. When the ring falls out of his pocket, Alex's friend, Brian picks up the ring off the floor. Heather sees Brian on his knees with the ring and believes he is proposing and she accepts the unintended proposal.

Of course, we don't know yet, if Heather will actually marry Brian. Does all this seem a bit confusing to you? It does to me. Probably by now you recognize the plot of Heather's story as the season finale of *Friends*, an NBC sitcom, that aired in May 2002. This episode of *Friends* was seen by 34.9 million viewers and was the most watched episode of any prime time series during the 2001-2002 season.[1]

With that many viewers watching *Friends*, it is a safe bet that some teens in our youth groups watched it as well. If our teens are watching *Friends*, we have to ask what are they learning about sex and dating? They learn:

- Peers admire someone who gets drunk and has sex.
- A dating relationship isn't necessary for sex or marriage.
- A marital relationship is optional for sexual fulfillment and parenting.
- Promiscuous behavior doesn't have negative spiritual or emotional consequences since Heather is happy having a baby.
- A couple can become so overcome by their sexual passion that they have sex in a janitor's closet.

Admittedly, we acknowledge that these are not the values we want teens learning, yet our culture generally accepts and promotes these values. Teens interact with the media's analysis of culture daily. The average teenager watches approximately 22 hours of television a week.[2] By the time members of our youth groups graduate from high school, they will have watched approximately fifteen thousand hours of television compared to the eleven thousand hours they have spent in a classroom.[3] The average teenager will listen to 10,500 hour of music from seventh grade to twelfth grade.[4] While music tastes vary widely, it is difficult to find a musical genre favored by teens that doesn't have lyrics that are sexually suggestive, if not sexually explicit.[5] Like it or not, the media impacts how teens view dating and sexuality.

If we don't acknowledge the influence of media and address it with members of our youth groups, we are silently endorsing media as the teacher of Sex Ed 101. When we don't provide information about sexuality to our teens, the media will. Even when we provide sex information, teens will be exposed continuously to media sexuality messages.

Media Dating Lessons 101

After a youth group devotional, Jose, a senior in high school, is sitting talking with Gary, a seventh grader, and John, an eighth grader. Jose talking about dating.

"When I'm on a date, I watch the red lights and the green lights," says Jose.

"What do you mean?" asks Gary.

"When I pick a girl up on a date, I look at what she is wearing. If it is a tight, sexy outfit, that's my first green light. Then if we go out to eat, I tell a dirty joke or make a sexual comment. If she laughs, that's my second green light. Then I reach under the table and caress her leg, if she doesn't pull away, that's a green light."

"What's a green light?"

"A green light means that she wants to have sex. A red light means she doesn't want to have sex."

"You can tell on a date that a girl wants to have sex by how she dresses and if she laughs at a dirty joke?"

"Usually you can tell. Because if a girl doesn't want to have sex with you, when you put an arm around her or you tell a dirty joke, she will let you know she's not interested. During the movie, I keep an arm around her and when we drive home, I keep a hand on her leg. If she lets me put an arm around her and keep a hand on her leg, that's another green light. If I have gotten all those green lights, I know we are going to make out and maybe even have sex."

"Even if you both want to have sex, where do you go?"

"I'll find a quiet place to pull off the road before we get to her house and I'll see how far she'll let me go. If she seems unsure about having sex, I tell her how special she is and how much I love her. I tell her that touching her is my way of showing her how much I love her."

"That really works?" asks John.

"I don't always have sex with her on the first date, but usually by the third date, we have sex. If we don't have sex by third or fourth date, I don't ask her out any more."

Jose didn't know that Sharon, a volunteer in the youth program overheard his conversation. Sharon is stunned. Jose is one of the most active teens in the youth group. She doesn't even know how to respond to what she has heard. Her immediate response is to tell Jose, Gary, and John that it is time to go home because she doesn't know what to say to Jose.

Although Jose's calculating strategies for initiating sexual activities on a date are contrary to biblical teachings, it should not surprise us that teens have beliefs like Jose's. In the absence of biblical teaching, our culture and the media define dating relationships. Our culture and the media teach that:

- Dating is a process for selecting sexual partners and fulfilling sexual desires.
- Dating allows experimentation with multiple sex partners.
- Dating doesn't lead to marriage, since marriage is an unnecessary commitment for sex.
- Having sex is the way to find love.
- Sex occurs naturally without any problems or embarrassments.
- There aren't negative spiritual or emotional consequences to having sex outside of marriage.
- All affection and touching must culminate in sex.
- If you aren't sexually active, you aren't attractive.
- Sexual urges are feelings of affection, love, and respect for one another.
- Being in a homosexual relationship is a viable option.
- You don't get pregnant or become infected with STDs when sexually active.

Based on our culture, dating becomes a selfish endeavor concerned with getting one's own needs met. Teens select dating partners based on physical attraction or social status. Dating popular peers can make it more likely that a peer group will accept teens. Similarly, dating may allow teens to attend social activities they would not otherwise attend. For example, dating an older student may allow a student to attend a prom or high school banquet. Sadly, some teens like Jose believe dating is only about initiating a sexual relationship.

Unhealthy Dating Relationships

Unhealthy dating relationships are characterized by:
- Centering on a sexual relationship
- No clear understanding of mutual boundaries and expectations
- One of the teens is jealous or possessive
- Teens become isolated from their friends and families
- Teens radically change their behavior or how they dress
- One of the teens makes all the decisions in the relationship
- No concern for the spiritual welfare of one another
- No real development of a healthy emotional relationship

Spiritual Dating Lessons 101

Although Sharon was initially stunned at what she heard Jose telling Gary and John about the green lights and red lights for having sex in a dating relationship, she decided that it was important to have a talk with Jose, Gary, and John directly. In talking with Jose, Gary, and John, she emphasized how important it was to develop spiritual and emotional aspects of a relationship rather than focusing on the sexual aspects of a relationship.

After discussing the situation with the youth ministry team, it was agreed that if Jose continued to encourage other teens in the youth group to have sex that they would ask him not to attend the social activities. Although they were willing to remove him from contact with other church teens, he did not continue to talk to the other teens about having sex while dating.

The youth ministry team decided to develop a series of lessons about dating to address the inappropriate dating information the media and peers share with church teens. The lessons were developed to emphasize spiritual principles in dating.

Unlike the dating relationships portrayed in the media, Christian dating relationships emphasize a concern for the welfare of others. Rather than the relationship focusing on sexual activities and social status, dating relationships focus on:

- **Gender differences.** Dating allows teens to learn about the differences between men and women.
- **Decision-making.** Frequently, dating relationships are one of the ways that teens first begin to make independent decisions with some limited guidance from their parents. Teens learn to accept the consequences of decision-making.
- **Companionship.** In a marriage relationship, partners spend more time involved in companionship activities than they do in sexual activities. Learning the social skills necessary for sharing common interests and providing companionship can be developed in a dating relationship.
- **Communication skills.** Teens learn to listen to their dates and reflect back meaning and emotional content of verbal messages in healthy dating relationships. They also learn to express their thoughts and feelings effectively.
- **Conflict-resolution skills.** All relationships eventually have some level of conflict. Teens can learn healthy conflict-resolution skills through dating

relationships. They can learn to express their opinions, assert their concerns, and compromise without alienating someone in a relationship.

■ **Setting boundaries.** In a dating relationship, teens learn to set emotional, physical, and sexual boundaries. They learn that they have a responsibility to protect themselves from people who ignore their boundaries.

■ **Emotional intimacy.** The give-and-take of disclosing intimate emotional concerns is a learning process. Knowing how much intimate information to disclose at what point in a relationship requires experience.

■ **Social activities.** Teens need a chance to engage in social activities. Dating can provide opportunities for participating in positive opportunities for peer interaction.

■ **Spiritual encouragement.** Dating relationships provide an opportunity to share spiritual concerns and to encourage each other's spiritual development.

■ **Marital partner.** Ultimately dating is a way for teens to determine what characteristics they desire in a marital partner. Dating lets teens learn about different personality characteristics and the roles of emotional intimacy and spiritual encouragement in a relationship.

Sending Red Lights
Guidelines for Teens

■ **Set clear limits.** If a date initiates physical or sexual contact, clearly remove yourself from the contact. Tell your date that you are not going to engage in sexual behavior.

■ **Plan dates.** Dates should center on social activity not sexual contact. Plan your dates so that you will be around other people and be involved in activities.

■ **Go dutch.** If allowing a date to pay for your meal or activities makes you feel like you owe them sexual access, then pay your own way. Don't place yourself in a situation where you feel like you owe your date sexual favors.

■ **Provide your own transportation.** Meet your date for an activity rather than having your date pick you up in a car. By driving your own car or having an adult provide transportation, you can avoid the temptation of engaging in sexual activities when you are alone in a car with a date.

■ **Group date.** Rather than having the pressure of spending exclusive time alone with date, get together with friends in a group for dating activities.

■ **Be assertive.** Don't agree to go places or engage in activities that make you uncomfortable. Be willing to express your opinion and to leave situations that make you uncomfortable. If a date ignores what you are saying, leave the situation immediately.

- **Don't drink or use drugs.** When you use drugs or alcohol, you are reducing your awareness of your surroundings and your ability to react quickly. Drugs and alcohol reduce your inhibitions about sex. Stay sober so you can maintain your boundaries.
- **No sexual comments.** If your date makes a sexual joke or lewd comment, tell them that you don't appreciate the comment or joke. Make it clear that you don't think sexual comments are appropriate on a date.
- **Modest clothing and behavior.** Wearing sexy and tight fitting clothing tells your date that you are interested in sex. When you dress modestly, you are setting a boundary and communicating that you respect your own body.
- **Don't send mixed messages.** When you laugh at sexual comments or allow your date to fondle you, you are sending a message that you are interested in a sexual relationship. Even if you are saying you aren't interested in sex, your behavior is communicating that you are interested in sex.
- **Don't go to secluded areas.** Your willingness to go to secluded places alone with your date indicates that you are interested in a sexual relationship. Secluded places can include spending time alone in a parked car or going to one of your homes when your parents aren't home.
- **Trust your gut feelings.** If something makes you uncomfortable or you don't like something that is going on, leave. You don't have to have a logical reason for ending a date if the date makes you feel uncomfortable.
- **Realize sex is not love.** Don't fall for lines like "you would if you loved me." Love involves companionship, emotional intimacy, and spiritual closeness, not just sex.

The Challenge

The challenge for youth workers in addressing dating concerns is in contesting the concepts the media and our culture teach about dating. While our culture promotes dating as an opportunity to experiment sexually and to engage in sexual relationships with multiple partners, the Bible calls us to engage in sexual relationships only in the context of a marriage. We must teach teens that dating is an opportunity for personal growth and exploration unrelated to sexual activities.

Similarly, our culture uses dating as an opportunity to establish status and popularity within a peer group. Yet dating in a Christian context is about learning to share emotional intimacy and spiritual encouragement. Our teens need to know that dating is much more complex than a popularity contest. God creates us in his image. Dating is an opportunity to see God's image in the lives of others.

RESPONDING TO THE CHALLENGE

1. What are some of the lessons teens learn about sex and dating when they watch TV?

_____

_____

_____

_____

2. What characteristics would indicate an unhealthy dating relationship?

_____

_____

_____

_____

3. If teens are involved in healthy dating relationships, what will they learn in the dating process?

_____

_____

_____

_____

4 What are some ways a teen can send clear messages to his/her dating partners that he/she will abstain from sexual contact on a date?

_____

_____

_____

_____

5

Stop! Don't Stop! Stop!

Elisha looks around a crowded room. She feels uncomfortable because she doesn't know anyone. She didn't want to move to a new city, but her dad got a promotion. Her parents told her that she would adjust, but they didn't understand how hard it was to fit into a new school and a new youth group. Now as she looks at strangers in a new youth group, she wants to be anywhere but here on a Wednesday evening.

While the youth minister gets up and begins to talk about the week's activities, Elisha sinks deeper into her chair. After several announcements, the youth minister sends the junior high teens to another room for their class. Elisha pries herself out of the chair and joins the other kids leaving the room. When Elisha reaches the door, she glances down to the classroom the other kids are entering and then looks back at the door leading out to the parking lot.

Her parents won't know if she skips class as long as she meets them after church in the foyer. She looks back at the other teens walking to the classroom. There aren't any adults watching them. She decides that next week she'll attend class, but this week she will wait outside.

She walks hurriedly toward the door to the parking lot, quietly opens the door, and slips into the darkness outside. She doesn't want anyone to see her, so she walks around to the side of the building. She sits on the curb of the sidewalk and waits. After a few minutes, she hears muffled voices. She listens to the rumbling of voices for a few minutes and decides to see who else is outside.

Elisha walks toward the back of the building. When she turns the corner, she sees three guys standing facing the wall. All three guys have their pants unzipped and are masturbating. Startled,

Elisha turns away to leave, but one of the guys has all ready seen her. He calls her over and explains that they are having an ejaculation contest. As she walks over, the guys zip their pants. He assures her they will stop if she won't tell anyone what they are doing. She agrees not to tell anyone what she has seen and stays to talk with the guys until their Bible study is over.

Those three guys become three of her best friends at church and school. They continue to cut out of Bible study and sneak to the back of the building. Initially, Elisha "judges" the ejaculation contests, but eventually they experiment with other sexual activities. During the next two years, their sexual activities evolve and escalate.

By the time Elisha is in high school, she is regularly having sex with multiple partners and is experimenting heavily with drugs and alcohol. However, she continues to excel in honors classes and actively attends church activities. Her parents and youth workers aren't aware that she is leaving these activities to engage in sex and use drugs. Generally, she stays on the premises where the church activity occurs. She leaves with friends and returns to the activity. If someone questions her absence, she has a plausible answer for her absence.

An unbelievable fictional story? Hardly. When I met Elisha as a young adult, she was struggling with drug use and was heavily involved in violent sexual activities with multiple male and female partners. She had no sense of boundaries about her sexual activities. Her parents and youth workers were stunned when as a young adult she dropped out of church and moved in with a drug dealer. They still were unaware of her history of sexual activities and drug use.

Elisha's story illustrates the difficulty teens have in establishing sexual boundaries. Initially, Elisha was an observer of sexual activity who agreed to keep a secret. Eventually Elisha became a participant who was willing to experiment with all types of sexual activity. Deciding to participate in sexual activities with multiple partners was a gradual process. Elisha illustrates how crossing one boundary leads to crossing another boundary and so on.

Inevitably, a discussion of sexual boundaries seems to revolve around the question of how far is far enough. Too often our answers are vague generalities like "It's different for everyone" and "You'll know when you've gone to far." The problem with these generalities is that teens have to go too far to find out what too far is. We are actually teaching stop, don't stop, stop. We are saying don't have sex, go far enough to know what is too far, then don't have sex. When teens go too far, they remove a boundary that is difficult to rebuild.

Boundaries for Sexual Activity

Even talking about having boundaries for sexual activity is contrary to cultural norms. Our culture teaches that sex defines male and female relationships. Sex sells. Sex defines happiness. Sex is the key to fulfillment and success. Our teens are trying to set sexual boundaries in a culture that sells sex as the defining component of identity. Our challenge is to help teens define their identity in a relationship with God rather than buying into the illusion that sex defines identity.

If we are going to help teens develop an accurate, godly perspective about sex, we have to define sex. Traditionally, we have told teens "don't do it," but we haven't defined "it." If we define "it" as intercourse, we may be inadvertently giving teens permission to engage in any sexual activity that is not intercourse. Literally, teens may engage in oral sex because they see it as a safe alternative to intercourse. From a physical perspective, they believe that oral sex doesn't have the danger of STDs and pregnancy. From a spiritual perspective, they don't believe that engaging in oral sex is wrong because it's not intercourse. If teens limit the definition of sex to intercourse, they have permission to engage in anything except intercourse. Intercourse is a culminating event. Sex is a process.

What Is Sex?

The sexual process includes:
- Everything leading up to or resulting from intercourse
- Everything we see or touch that stimulates sexual arousal
- Lustful thoughts, the longing to unite, the emotional commitment
- Passionate kisses, heavy petting, and foreplay
- Pornography, explicit fantasy, and self-arousal
- An internal process leading up to sexual arousal
- An interpersonal process leading to the union of two people
- Anything that has the potential to result in intercourse or masturbation.[1]

Once sex is defined as a process, it is easier to help teens begin to consider boundaries for sexual activity. When teens ask, "How far is too far?" they may be asking for information they don't know about the process of sexual behavior. Teens who don't recognize anything except intercourse as sex are vulnerable to engaging in other sexual behaviors. Presenting a continuum of sexual contact for teens as part of the discussion of sexuality may be helpful. Too often teens are given information about reproduction, but not information about sexual behaviors leading up to intercourse. In fact, teens may have more information about the consequences of sex (pregnancy and STDs) than they have about sex itself. The following chart presents information about the physical continuum of sexual behavior.

Continuum of Sexual Contact

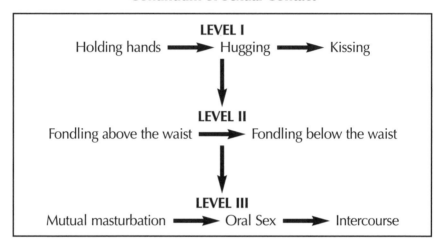

Obviously, teens are going to have sexual thoughts and urges because they are experiencing puberty and because God created all of us as sexual beings. The challenge for youth workers is helping teens distinguish between normal sexual urges and thoughts and becoming involved in sexual behaviors that are only appropriate in a marital relationship. As teens leave Level I behaviors and become involved in Level II behaviors, they are engaging in behaviors that are only appropriate in a marital relationship.

While as adults we would probably agree in general terms with this continuum, teens are likely to view a sexual continuum quite differently.

Teens may even believe

"You aren't having sex if you wear a condom."

"You aren't having sex if you don't have an orgasm during intercourse."

"Oral sex isn't sex."

"Anything that doesn't lead to having a baby isn't sex."

Teens would probably rework the continuum of sexual behavior in an entirely different manner. Their continuum might look like the following:

Teen View of Sexual Contact		
NOT SEX...	Holding hands	Hugging
	Kissing	Fondling above the waist
	Fondling below the waist	Mutual masturbation
	Oral Sex	
SEX...	Intercourse	

In today's youth culture, teens don't necessarily view sexual activity as progressive. They view all sexual activity, except for intercourse, as not having "sex." Intercourse is the only activity that is "sex." This view of sexuality endorses all sexual activities, except for intercourse. In fact, teens would view holding hands and oral sex as being equally intimate and permissible. Oral sex is a preferred sexual activity because teens believe it is without risk. They believe that they can't get pregnant and they can't get STDs from oral sex when actually they can catch STDs through oral sex. If we are going to address boundaries in teen sexuality, we have to help teens recognize the progressive aspects of a continuum of sexual activity. In discussing a continuum of sexual behavior, we have to clearly define what sexual behaviors are only appropriate in marriage.

One of the challenges in discussing boundaries with teens is frequently teens will already be involved in fondling, mutual masturbation, and oral sex. It may be difficult to persuade these teens that their current behavior is inappropriate sexual contact outside the confines of a marriage. Even if we persuade these teens that their behavior is inappropriate, it will be a struggle for them to change their sexual boundaries in dating relationships. The goal of teaching about boundaries is to help teens get back to Level I behaviors and help them abstain from Level II and Level III behaviors before marriage.

Spiritual and Emotional Consequences

In addition to understanding the physical continuum of sexual behavior, it is equally important that teens understand the emotional and spiritual consequences of sexual behavior. As teens move from hugging, kissing, and holding hands to other sexual behaviors, there are emotional and spiritual consequences. Sexual behavior creates an emotional bond between two people and connects them in a way no other behavior connects two people. Sex allows a person to have intimate knowledge of another person physically and emotionally. Any sexual activity requires trust to some degree on the part of both people because sexual activities inherently create vulnerability. The vulnerability of sexual relationships frequently leads couples to make decisions about their relationship based on a connection found in sex rather than making decisions based on their relationship with God.

Teens who have sex with multiple partners will argue that sex doesn't create a bond between them and their sexual partner. However, if teens have reached the point where sex does not create a bond with their sexual partner, they have lost their ability to trust and be vulnerable in a sexual relationship. Instead of trusting their sexual partner, they maintain as much control as possible in any sexual encounter and intentionally engage in behaviors preventing emotional intimacy. Teens who have lost this ability to trust in a sexual relationship frequently begin to use drugs, mutilate themselves, and take risks with their lives because sex isn't fulfilling their need for acceptance and intimacy. They are emotionally and spiritually isolated and engaging in sexual behaviors that don't produce intimacy.

Teens who choose intimate sexual contact outside of marriage experience spiritual consequences. More and more frequently teens tell me that they are sexually active because it feels good. These teens are worshiping sexual pleasure rather than worshiping God. They have chosen their own physical pleasure over their relationship with God. Similarly, teens who are seeking emotional acceptance and fulfillment through a sexual relationship are looking in the wrong place to have their needs met. These teens are engaging in sexual behavior because they want to "be loved." They are choosing an imitation of love rather than choosing the love that God offers them.

Warning: No Relationship Required

Most of the discussions in this book have approached sexual issues as though the teens are involved in a dating relationship. The reality is that teens may engage in sexual activities without having an emotional or dating relationship with their sexual partners. It would be naïve and misguided to assume that most teen sexual activity occurs in the context of relationships. The biggest challenge we may face in talking about sexual activities with some teens is putting sex in the context of any relationship, much less a marital relationship. As difficult as it is for us to comprehend, teens may view sexual activity as nothing more than a physical event.

Knowing Where the Line Is

While teens may argue that they don't know where the boundaries are for sexual behavior in a dating relationship, they have no similar difficulties defining appropriate sexual behavior for a married couple. Ask teens to imagine that their mother is married and has taken a new job. Since she has started her new job, she has developed a personal relationship with her boss. Her new boss is an attractive and charismatic man who is slightly younger than their mother. Their mother and her boss have begun to spend more time together. They frequently work on the same projects and attend luncheon meetings together. They have begun meeting some on weekends to work on projects. Would it be okay for their mom to kiss her boss? Hold his hand? Hug him? Generally, when teens are asked these questions, they are quick to indicate that no physical contact is appropriate. If teens can so easily define appropriate boundaries for a sexual relationship within a marriage, they can also define appropriate boundaries for sexual relationships outside of marriage.

How Do We Help Teens Set Boundaries?

■ **Talk about sex.** We have to talk about sex as a process, not as a culminating event. In talking about sex as a process, we have to talk about various types of sexual activity and how engaging in one type of behavior can lead to another behavior.

■ **Go counterculture.** Help teens recognize that our culture is selling sex as the integral component of identity. Counter to what our culture teaches, our identity is found in our relationship with God.

■ **Draw a line in the sand.** Be willing to say to teens that sexual behaviors are wrong and hold them accountable for changing their behavior. They don't want us to endorse their behavior. They want us to teach them right from wrong and to confront them when they are involved in sexual behavior.

■ **Get with the group.** Provide opportunities for teens to be involved in activities with peers when they are dating. Spending time alone together as a couple sets teens up to engage in sexual behavior.

■ **Rules rule.** Have established guidelines for acceptable and unacceptable physical contact between teens in the youth group.

■ **Zero tolerance.** Don't allow sexual harassment, whether verbal or nonverbal, to occur in the youth group.

■ **On alert.** Have chaperones for all church activities and require teens to stay in specific assigned locations. Don't let teens wander off by

---

themselves during youth group activities. Don't let teens have exclusive time alone with peers on overnight activities or out-of-town trips.

- **No experience required.** Encourage teens to avoid sexual experimentation and to wait until marriage to engage in sexual behaviors.
- **Swimming suit rule.** Teach teens not to touch other people where their swimming suit would be and not to put their hands under someone's clothes. Teens also need to know it is not appropriate to get in a prone position with another teen.
- **Forgiveness available.** Help teens engaging in sexual behavior to realize that God will forgive them.
- **How good is good enough?** Encourage teens to spend their time thinking of the good they can do with their lives rather than spending their time considering how far they can go in a sexual relationship without going too far.[2]
- **Accountability.** Be willing to hold teens accountable for their sexual purity. Check in with them to make sure that they are setting healthy sexual boundaries.

Extra Caution: Drugs and Alcohol

Drinking and using drugs can reduce inhibitions and a teen's ability to make good decisions. When teens drink or use drugs they have a distorted sense of their surroundings, are unable to set clear sexual boundaries, and may not recognize dangerous situations. Quite literally, being intoxicated or high may reduce a teen's ability to physically or verbally resist sex.

Teens must be cautious if they attend activities where drugs or alcohol are used. Obviously, in some situations, teens will recognize that their peers are using drugs or alcohol. However, teens may also find themselves attending activities where they don't realize teens are using drugs and alcohol.

Safety Precautions for Teens

- Avoid drinking or using drugs.
- Don't accept food or drinks from people you don't know.
- Attend activities that have adult chaperones.
- Don't go to parties with teens you don't know.
- Be sure an adult is aware of where you are and when you should return.

Guard Your Conscience

Teens need help in establishing boundaries about sexual contact. We can encourage teens to develop their conscience concerning sex through several different approaches.

When teens are faced with making decisions about sexual behavior, have them imagine their unborn children sitting on one shoulder watching every action and knowing it will affect their future. On the other shoulder, have them imagine Jesus watching them. They need to think about what activities they would participate in if their own children were watching? If Jesus was watching? Would they kiss their date? Sure. Would they go further? Not so clear … danger![3]

Similarly, when teens begin to think that the sexual aspects of their relationship are becoming more important than the spiritual aspects of their relationship, have them stop whatever they are doing and pray with their date. If a dating relationship is reaching the point where teens aren't able to stop at any moment and ask their date to pray with them, then they need to stop what they are doing. If at any point, stopping to pray would be awkward then the sexual contact has gone too far. However, if stopping to pray is acceptable at any given moment, then the sexual boundaries in the relationship are probably okay.[4]

The Challenge

A generation or two ago, teens talked about getting to first base, second base, or third base before getting a home run. These teens clearly understood that removing sexual boundaries was a progressive activity. Today's teens don't seem to be as aware of the progression of sexual activities.[5] When we are teaching abstinence, teens are hearing "don't do it." When teens hear "don't do it," they interpret our teaching to mean they can do anything sexual as long as they don't have intercourse.

Our challenge is to help teens recognize that sex is a progressive activity. As they allow one boundary to fall, another boundary quickly follows. We need to be able to clearly communicate to teens that there are lines that shouldn't be crossed prior to marriage. While talking about purity is essential, it is no longer specific enough for today's teens. Our teens need for us to clearly define the progression of sexual activities and clearly state what specific behaviors are inappropriate.

RESPONDING TO THE CHALLENGE

1. Why is it is essential to present sexuality as a process, not an event?

_____
_____
_____
_____

2. In working with our youth groups, what should we talk about instead of "how far is too far?"

_____
_____
_____
_____

3. What are some of the consequences for teens if they have sex before they are married?

_____
_____
_____
_____

4. What are some strategies we can use to help teens learn to set appropriate sexual boundaries in relationships?

_____
_____
_____
_____

SECTION THREE
HANDLING
CHALLENGING ISSUES

The *focus* of this section of the book is to help you recognize the symptoms and characteristics of teens struggling with sexual issues. Each of the chapters describes one or more sexual issues, symptoms, and warning signs.

The *purpose* in each chapter is to offer strategies for helping teens deal with sexual issues: pornography, pregnancy, dating violence, sexual abuse, and homosexuality. While youth workers will not routinely deal with these issues, they will deal with some or all of these issues at different times in a youth group. Each chapter is designed to stand alone and can be referenced when needed.

We have to deal with our own
insecurities and anxieties
about sex if we are going
to provide guidance and
mentoring for teens.
When we are no longer afraid
of talking to teens about sex,
we will be effective.

6

Pornography

A mission trip to an inner-city church was Barbara's idea. She campaigned for the youth program to spend a week in the inner-city church and provide a vacation Bible school program for the children of the neighborhood. Barbara's brother was the minister in an inner-city church, and Barbara knew how much he needed help with his ministry.

After a year of planning the youth volunteers took fifteen teens to teach the VBS. The teens spent the nights at the church and worked together to prepare meals. There wasn't much free time. In addition to teaching VBS classes that were overflowing with children, the teens did some painting and maintenance work in the church building. Amazingly, there were no major conflicts in the group and everyone seemed to be working together as a team.

After a week of working with the inner-city ministry, the teens seemed more committed to their Christian faith and more compassionate toward others. When the missions team returned home, Barbara felt affirmed in her belief in the inner-city mission and believed her local church would make a long-term commitment to the ministry.

Barbara is stunned when the church gets a letter from inner-city ministry leaders detailing hundreds of dollars of long-distance phone charges that were made while the mission team was staying in the church building. Most of the long-distance charges were for a telephone sex line. When the church leaders met with the mission team, everyone denied making the phone calls. The church leaders agreed to pay the phone charges, but demanded that all the procedures for out-of-town trips be reviewed.

Barbara is heartbroken and disillusioned. She believed that these teens were committed in their faith. They were the most actively involved teens in the youth group. During the months following the mission trip, Barbara becomes even more disillusioned when teens gradually began talking to church leaders and youth volunteers. Unknown to the parents and youth volunteers, several of the core members of the youth group had been involved in pornography for several years.

Beginning in fifth grade, one of the kids began taking porn magazines from his father and brought them to church activities to show the other kids. Gradually the teens had gained access to pornography online and on video. When teens had been gathering at each other's homes to hang out, they had been viewing porn online or on video in their rooms. They had accessed telephone sex lines using phone cards or making phone calls on other people's phones. Now as high school students, several of the teens had developed a serious problem with pornography.

While all of us would like to believe that this story is a sensationalized narrative used to grab your attention, it is a true story. Some of the details have been changed to allow the congregation involved to have some anonymity, but it is true. I personally have no difficulty believing the story because when a foster child living in my home was in fifth grade, the other kids in his class at school threatened him with bodily harm if he told anyone that they had porn magazines stashed in their lockers. Those kids threatening him were from good church-going families who had no clue what their kids were involved in at school. The average age for a child to be exposed to pornography is eleven,[1] which means some children are exposed even younger than eleven.

It shouldn't surprise us that our teens are exposed to pornography when there are more hard-core pornography stores than McDonald's restaurants in the U.S.[2] In 1996, people spent more than $8 billion on hard-core pornography which is more money than was generated by Hollywood's domestic box office receipts that year.[3] Similarly, in the same year, more money was spent at strip clubs than at the theater, the opera, the ballet, and jazz, and classical performances.[4] It is an understatement to say that pornography is big business. Teens are impacted by the big business of pornography. Phone companies estimate that minors make 70% of the 500,000 daily calls to pornographic telephone lines.[5] Similarly, it is estimated that 70% of all pornographic magazines and videos eventually make their way to the hands of children.[6]

Pornographic Materials Include:

- Internet Web sites
- Pornographic magazines
- Adult cable programming
- Hard-core pornography

- Telephone sex lines
- Peep shows
- Live sex acts
- Strip clubs

The easiest way for teens to access pornography is the Internet. On average, a teen uses the Internet four days a week for two hours at a time,[7] and three out of four teens use the Internet.[8] When teens are online, three out of four of them are using instant messaging technology where they can be contacted by strangers and invited to view pornographic material online. Similarly, teens entering chat rooms can be targeted by individuals seeking a sexual relationship. A recent study found that one in five minors between the ages of 10 and 17 have been solicited for sex over the Internet in the last year.[9]

Teens have the distinction of growing up in a time when the Internet allows unparalleled access to pornography.[10,11,12] Online e-mail boxes can be inundated with pornographic materials, while Web sites offer immediate access to sexually explicit material. Playboy's Web site which offers free glimpses of playmates, now averages about five million hits a day.[13] The newest generation of pornography allows personal computer users to disrobe images of women and use simulated sex toys on them.[14] Even if teens accidentally stumble upon a pornographic Web site, they may be trapped by the a new marketing technique that prevents people from exiting out of the Web site.[15]

Teens engaging in pornographic activities may not be "caught" and may find it difficult to discuss their behavior with others. To outsiders, teens viewing pornography may seem to be committed Christians. They may hide their propensity for pornography for years. If they confess their interest in pornography, they may lose their status in the youth group, and their parents and families may be disappointed in them.

What Does Pornography Depict?

- Nudity
- Heterosexual activities
- Homosexual activities
- Violent sexual activities
- Group sex

- Child pornography
- Incest pornography
- Sex with animals
- Sexual activities intended to humiliate[16]

Effects of Pornography

Viewing pornography can affect attitudes toward women and sex, as well as impacting a teen's spiritual life. Teens use pornography to arouse themselves when they are masturbating. In addition, teens viewing pornography engage in other behaviors that are modeled in the pornography. Pornography will lead to teens having distorted perceptions about sex. They may begin to have an interest in more deviant, bizarre, or violent types of pornography.[17] Once they develop an interest in viewing these types of pornography, they will develop an interest in engaging in these types of sexual activity.

Teens who view pornography believe that having sex with multiple partners outside of a marriage relationship is normal. As a result, they don't see the value of marriage and monogamous sexual relationships.[18] Teenage males viewing pornography develop callousness toward women so extreme that rape is trivialized. Ultimately, and most significantly, pornography creates a chasm between God and the teen. Teens become focused on sexual pleasure and their desires promoting selfishness, rather than focusing on God's will for their lives. They put their time, energy, and money into seeking sexual pleasure, rather than putting their time and energy into developing a relationship with God.

Interestingly, some teens use their Christian values to rationalize pornography use.[19] Teens who are not engaging in sexual intercourse may believe that watching pornography is a consolation activity. These teens tell themselves that watching pornography is better than engaging in sexual intercourse, so it is okay for them to view pornography. This argument becomes especially validated when teens have Christian friends who are having sex with multiple partners. We have to help teens recognize that viewing pornography is not a substitute activity for sex if they are committed to abstinence. We have to help teens understand that their focus needs to be on developing a relationship with God, not on seeking sexual pleasure.

How Serious Is This?

Determining how involved a teen is with pornographic activities is essential. Certainly, we don't want our teens to be using pornography in any way, but how we respond to a teen's involvement with pornography needs to be based on the type of involvement the teen has with the pornographic world. For example, a teen feeling guilt and remorse because he looked at a porn magazine one time in a locker room is a much different situation than a teen viewing pornography online every afternoon for two years. While both teens need assistance in dealing with their actions, they need different types of assistance. The following questions can be used to assess teen pornography use.

Assess the Situation

- How long have you been viewing pornography?
- How often do you view pornography?
- How are you accessing pornography?
- Do other people know you view pornography?
- How much time do you spend viewing pornography?
- How much money are you spending on pornography?
- Are you spending more time viewing pornography than you have before?
- Is pornography affecting your schoolwork or friendships?

As you consider teen answers to these questions, there are some red flags to watch for. First, if the teen has been viewing pornography for an extended period of time and on a regular basis, it may be a difficult habit to break. Second, if the teen is using a considerable amount of time and money to view pornography, the behavior may be deeply engrained. Third, it may be difficult for teens to find activities to replace viewing pornography if they have become isolated in their use of pornography. Finally, the use of pornography may have led to involvement in other sexual behaviors that require professional assistance.

Dealing with Pornography Use

Louis isn't happy about living with his grandparents. His mother has cancer and is so weak she can't take care of herself, so they moved back into his grandparents' house. His mother told him they would live with his grandparents until she got stronger. He isn't going to make friends at his new school because that means he believes he might be staying at his new school. If he believes he might stay at his new school, then he would be accepting the possibility that his mother might not get well. He won't consider that possibility, so he goes to school and comes home and isolates himself at his grandparents' house.

Initially, his grandparents let him set up his computer, but they didn't have Internet access. After several weeks of isolating himself, his mother urged his grandparents to allow him to have

Internet access because she thought he might be happier if he could e-mail his friends from his previous school. Louis began e-mailing friends and using instant messaging to catch up on what was happening in his former school, but he still had a lot of time in the evenings and on the weekends. He began surfing the net and gradually began viewing porn sites. Since his computer was in his bedroom, no one knew he was viewing porn sites.

His grandparents and mother continued to worry about his isolation and lack of interest in participating in activities at school or at church. His grandparents call the church youth minister and ask him to make an extra effort to involve Louis in the youth activities. The youth minister, Jake, arranges with the grandparents to come by one evening to visit with Louis. During the first visit, Louis seemed detached and uninterested in talking with Jake; but Jake persisted and continued to drop by and see Louis in the evenings.

After several visits, Jake noticed that Louis' computer was on and asked what he was doing on the computer. Louis didn't answer initially and then said, "It's nothing you'd be interested in."

Jake began to suspect that Louis was involved in online activities that weren't appropriate, so every time he would visit with Louis, he would ask about his computer activities. Eventually, Louis told Jake that he had been surfing the Internet looking at pornography. Jake thought about talking with Louis' grandparents about ending Louis' access to the Internet, but Jake realized that Louis would probably find other ways to access pornography. Instead, Jake began to talk with Louis about why he was viewing pornography. Louis told Jake that, initially, he had viewed the pornography because he was bored, but once he had begun viewing the pornography, he enjoyed the sexual stimulation.

Louis didn't see anything wrong with viewing the pornography. He wasn't actually having sex with anyone and no one forced people to pose for pornographic pictures. Louis believed that it was better for him to be viewing pornography online instead of making out with a girl. Jake recognized that he would have to help Louis realize that viewing pornography was wrong if Louis was going to quit viewing it. One evening he had this conversation with Louis:

"Louis, do your grandparents and your mother know you are looking at pornography on the Internet?"

"No way. They'd go ballistic if they knew."

"Why would they be upset?"

"They would think it was wrong for me to be looking at porn."

"But you don't think it's wrong?"

"Well, it's not as wrong as other stuff I could be doing."

"So maybe it's a little wrong, but not really wrong?"

"Yeah. I could be going out and having sex and doing stuff myself. I'm just watching it. I'm not doing it."

"Does watching porn make you think about having sex yourself?"

"Yeah, I guess so, but I'm not doing it."

"In Matthew 5:28, Jesus says that anyone who looks at a woman lustfully has already committed adultery with her in his heart. Do you think that could apply to pornography?"

"Maybe it does, but it just gives me something to do."

At this point, Jake lets the topic of the conversation shift because he doesn't want to alienate Louis. Because he doesn't push Louis during this conversation, several other conversations follow. Eventually, Jake persuades Louis that looking at pornography is wrong. Louis agrees to tell Jake when he's struggling with his decision not to view pornography. Louis asks his grandparents to put the computer in the living room, so he can't surf the Internet alone in his bedroom. When Louis is tempted to surf the Internet, he calls Jake or takes a long walk to get him away from the computer.

Jake also encouraged Louis to get involved with youth group activities, so that he could develop some friendships with other kids his age. Jake helped Louis understand that his mother's health didn't depend on whether or not he made friends. As Louis began making friends in the youth group, he spent more time praying and studying his Bible. Although he occasionally is tempted to look at pornography, he is able to make his spiritual relationship his priority rather than relying on sexual stimulation to help him deal with his fears about his mother's illness. In helping Louis decide not to view pornography, Jake illustrates how to help teens struggling with pornography.

Knowing What to Do

■ **Knowing wrong from right.** If teens don't believe that viewing pornography is wrong or won't admit they are viewing pornography, then any other efforts to help them will be wasted.

■ **Accountability.** Teens need to be held accountable by an adult who will help them avoid looking at pornography. Teens need to be completely honest and admit when they are accessing pornography and how they are accessing pornography.

- **Clean it out.** Teens must get rid of all access to pornography at school, work, or home. Getting rid of porn means throwing out music containing sexually explicit lyrics and videos containing sexually explicit scenes. In addition, teens accessing pornography with a computer, don't need to surf the Internet when they are alone.

- **Get away.** When teens get in a situation where they are tempted to view pornography, they need to recognize the temptation and flee from it as quickly as possible. They need to avoid surfing the Internet and shopping in stores that sell porn magazines or sex videos.

- **Get a life.** Frequently, pornography occupies so much time that teens don't have hobbies and other interests to occupy them. Teens may need help planning time when they are alone, so they won't spend time viewing pornography.

- **Find some friends.** If pornography has been substituted for relationships because teens feel insecure, then teens may not have supportive relationships with peers and adults and may also feel lonely and isolated. Consequently, teens need help developing the skills they need to establish relationships with peers.

- **Get over the guilt.** Once teens acknowledge that pornography is wrong, they may feel a great deal of guilt about their behavior. Remind them that God loves them even if they don't believe they are worthy of his love. He loves them even when they sin.

- **Focus on faith.** Help teens recognize that they need to strengthen their relationship with God. By focusing on prayer and Bible study, they can turn their heart's desire toward God instead of sex.

- **Patience please.** Teach teens to be patient with their setbacks. It took time for them to develop an interest in pornography, it will take them time to overcome their interest in pornography.

In Over Your Head

As you consider what to do to help teens deal with pornography, recognize that there will be situations when you need to refer teens for professional counseling services to help them deal with pornography. If the answer to any of the following questions is yes, then you may need to refer the teen to a professional counselor.

- Has the teen tried to quit viewing pornography and has failed to quit?
- Is the teen continuing to increase the amount of time spent watching pornography?
- Is the teen viewing pornography on a regular basis for several hours a week?
- Is viewing pornographic material continuing to increase the frequency of masturbation?
- Is the teen watching other people undress or engage in sexual activities?
- Is the teen fantasizing about rape or other violent sexual behaviors?
- Is the teen videotaping himself having sex with other people?
- Is the teen involved in other inappropriate sexual behaviors?

The Challenge

The challenge in dealing with pornography is helping teens recognize that viewing pornography is wrong. Living in a culture that endorses sexually explicit media of all forms provides a constant temptation for viewing pornography. Pornography provides instant access to sexual images in a society teaching directly and indirectly sex leads to love and happiness.

Similarly, teens view pornography as a harmless form of recreation without victims. Teens believe viewing pornography is not harmful to themselves or anyone else. They don't recognize that viewing pornography impacts their views of sexuality and changes the way they relate to others in sexual relationships.

RESPONDING TO THE CHALLENGE

1. What are some ways teens can access pornography?

_____

_____

_____

_____

2. What do teens learn about sexuality when they view pornography?

_____

_____

_____

_____

3. If a teen is viewing pornography, what are some issues to consider when assessing the situation?

_____

_____

_____

_____

4. What can we do to help teens avoid pornography?

_____

_____

_____

_____

5. If a teen is viewing pornography, how can we help him or her quit?

_____

_____

_____

_____

7

Pregnancy and Other Issues

Julia generally arrived early for youth group activities and was quick to help the adults set up the room and the refreshments. During the past two years, Julia and Amanda, a youth volunteer, developed a mentoring relationship. Amanda thought she knew about the significant events in Julia's life. Admittedly, they had not been as close since Julia began dating Gerald six months ago, but Amanda was shocked to learn that she hadn't been aware of what was happening in Julia's life.

Before a Bible study on Sunday evening, Julia asked, "Can we talk for a few minutes?"

"Sure, Julia. What's going on?"

"Can we find some place away from everyone else to talk?"

"Yeah."

They walked down the hall where they could not be overheard, but other adults could still see them. Julia took a deep breath and blurted out, "I think I might be pregnant, but I'm not sure."

Amanda is surprised, but needs more information to decide how she can help Julia.

"Okay. You must be overwhelmed right now. Tell me why you think you are pregnant."

"I'm late. I haven't started my period and I'm nearly a month late."

"Sometimes your period can be late without your being pregnant. Have you been having intercourse with someone?"

Julia' face flushes red with embarrassment as she stammers, "Well ... um ... not exactly."

"What do you mean not exactly?"

"Well, we haven't been actually doing it, but we've gotten

pretty close to having sex."

"Has your sexual partner been ejaculating?"

Julia drops her eyes and responds, "Yeah."

"Well, you might be pregnant. Have you taken a pregnancy test?"

"No. "

"Before you get yourself panicked about being pregnant, you need to find out if you are actually pregnant. Let's talk about some options for determining if you are pregnant."

In responding to Julia, Amanda is providing reassurance and guidance concerning pregnancy. Amanda does not immediately respond as though Julia is pregnant since Julia does not have any medical proof of pregnancy. Instead of following Julia's lead in confirming a pregnancy, Amanda takes a few minutes to assess the situation.

Assess the Situation

- Why does the teen believe she is pregnant?
- Has the teen taken a home pregnancy test?
- Has the teen been to see a medical professional to confirm the pregnancy?
- Are the teen's parents aware of the pregnancy?
- Is the baby's father aware of the pregnancy?
- Who else is aware of the pregnancy?
- What does the teen plan to do about the pregnancy?

Once Amanda assesses the situation, she determines that the first step in assisting Julia is helping Julia determine if she is pregnant. In the initial conversation with a teen, you may need to provide different types of assistance based on how much information that teen has about pregnancy and who else is aware of the pregnancy.

The First Conversation

If, like Julia, the teen has not taken a home pregnancy test or talked with a medical professional, the teen may need assistance to determine if she is pregnant. You want to be cautious about how much involvement you have in helping a teen determine if she is pregnant. An obvious first step is for the teen to take a home pregnancy test, but home pregnancy tests are not as accurate as tests done in a medical clinic. It is likely that there is a medical clinic available in your area that provides free pregnancy testing or pregnancy testing for a reasonable fee.

As a general rule, you can provide information to a teen about available resources, but you probably don't want to transport a teen to a medical clinic or buy a home pregnancy test for the teen. While our inclination is to assist a teen in every way possible, we need to recognize that getting too involved in transporting a teen or helping a teen access medical care may be detrimental. If teens are old enough to voluntarily engage in sexual activities, then they are old enough to take responsibility for their actions. Similarly, if we assume too much responsibility in assisting the teen, she may delay telling her parents and the baby's father about the pregnancy. Certainly, we want to assist the teen in finding ways to access resources. If a teen needs transportation, we need to help him or her identify someone who can help them with transportation issues. Obviously, if a teen is pregnant due to sexual assault, we need to respond in a totally different way.

If a teen has taken a pregnancy test to confirm the pregnancy, then she likely will be asking for assistance with other issues in the pregnancy. One of the most common concerns a pregnant teen will have is how to tell her parents about the pregnancy. While teens are genuinely concerned about their parents' reactions and fear that their parents will react in a hostile or negative way, generally parents handle the situation well. However, if you have genuine concerns about how the parents will react, you might suggest that the teen have someone else accompany her to talk with her parents. In a few instances, you may have a teen who wants to discuss the possibility of having an abortion, so she won't have to discuss the situation with her parents.

Unplanned Pregnancies

Most teen pregnancies are unintentional and unplanned. Generally teens get pregnant either because they literally don't understand biologically how it is possible to get pregnant or because they choose to engage in unprotected sex. Although teens are saturated with sexual messages in the media and the culture, very few of these messages give good information about how pregnancy occurs. Characters in movies and television have sex with multiple partners without any consequences of pregnancy.

Some teens get pregnant because they don't understand how someone gets pregnant. A common misperception among sexually active teens is that the only way you can get pregnant is to have oral sex. These teens believe that pregnancy occurs when a sperm is swallowed. Believe it or not, these same teens sat in health classes and biology classes, but they have not connected the information they learned in health class with their behavior on dates. They sat in lectures about reproduction, but have not connected discussions about sperm and eggs with the vagina and penis.

A second misperception related to pregnancy is that the only way you can get pregnant is by a penis penetrating a vagina. Teens are unaware that intimate sexual contact leading to ejaculation without penetration may also result in pregnancy. A "splash pregnancy" occurs when seminal fluid penetrates the vaginal opening without vaginal intercourse. Once the seminal fluid enters the vagina, it swims up through the female reproductive system and fertilizes an egg causing pregnancy. Teens need to be aware that any time males ejaculate during sexual contact, there is a possibility for pregnancy to occur.[1]

Planned Pregnancies

While most teen pregnancies are unplanned,[2] it would be naïve to believe that all teen pregnancies are unplanned. There are teens intentionally trying to get pregnant. Teens may plan a pregnancy for any of the following reasons:

- **Escape.** Teens may want to leave their parents' homes and pregnancy is viewed as a way to establish independence from their parents.
- **Abuse.** Teens may get pregnant to stop a perpetrator from sexually abusing them. One in ten pregnancies is the result of a sexual assault, usually incest.[3]
- **Affection.** Teens may want unconditional love and they believe that a baby will love them.
- **Entrapment.** Teens may get pregnant because they want to marry their sexual partner and believe that if they get pregnant their sexual partner will marry them.
- **Status.** In certain groups of teens, having children is a way to establish status. Teen parents are respected for their virility within some groups.

Knowing What to Do
- **Take responsibility.** Teens who are pregnant need to recognize that they are going to have to make significant decisions about the life of a child. Whether teens choose abortion, adoption, or raising the child, there are significant consequences to their decisions.
- **Real parenting.** If teens believe that they want to raise the child

---

themselves, they need to have a realistic idea of the demands of parenting. They need to take parenting classes and need adults to introduce a realistic picture of taking care of a child 24 hours a day.

- **Selective inclusion.** While we don't want to exclude pregnant teens from youth group activities, we also need to make responsible choices. We don't want to include pregnant teens in activities that might result in physical harm to the baby. We can be held legally liable if we allow pregnant teens to participate in risky activities.
- **Connection with other parents.** Realistically, a pregnant teen needs assistance in making connections with other Christian parents who can mentor them. Although pregnant teens don't recognize how an infant will change their lives, they won't be participating in the same social circles if they are parenting a child. These teen parents will need connections with other parents once they have their child.
- **All or nothing.** If teens want to raise a child themselves, they need to recognize the enormity of the responsibility. As a general rule, when grandparents or other family members assume a great deal of the responsibility for raising the child, it eventually creates significant conflicts between the teen and the grandparents. Families split apart in custody battles over children or over disagreements in parenting. If a teen cannot parent the child themselves, grandparents or other family members need to either take legal custody of the child or encourage the teen to find a family to adopt the child.
- **Acceptance, not endorsement.** Teens who are pregnant certainly need support from their church family, but we need to balance the need for support with glamorizing pregnancy. Our culture does not place any stigma on pre-marital sex and having children outside a marriage relationship. We must balance our support of pregnant teens with what we model for other teens in the youth group. We don't want to indirectly endorse teen pregnancy.
- **Acknowledgment of wrongdoing.** Teens who are pregnant need to acknowledge that engaging in pre-marital sex is wrong. Without an acknowledgement of wrongdoing, teens may see nothing wrong with their actions. Once again we may be indirectly telling other members of the youth group that pre-marital sex is okay. Certainly, church leaders need to use wisdom and discernment in how they handle the situation. The exception to this would be if the teen was forced to engage in non-consensual sex.

Abortion

Krista is frequently rude and disrespectful when Alyssa, a youth volunteer, tries to interact with her at youth group activities. Other kids in the youth group are friendly toward Krista, but they don't interact with her outside structured youth group activities. Alyssa has tried to encourage the other teens to reach out to Krista, but the teens respond by telling Alyssa that Krista hangs out with kids who drink and use drugs.

One evening Krista is extremely defiant and rude during a class activity, so Alyssa calls her aside. Alyssa is angry and begins to lecture Krista. In response, Krista gets angry and responds, "You don't know what you are talking about."

"I do know what I'm talking about. You are being rude and disrespectful in class."

"So what! Why shouldn't I be rude? My parents make me come to church. I don't want to be here. I don't like being a hypocrite."

Although Alyssa is angry, she recognizes that Krista is talking about more than her inappropriate class behavior.

"Maybe I don't know what I'm talking about."

Krista, still angry, responds, "That's right. You don't know anything about me."

"What don't I know about you?"

"You don't know that I killed my babies. You don't know that I still hear them crying at night. You don't know that my mom and dad didn't give me a choice. You don't know that everyone in my family is a hypocrite."

"What do you mean that you killed your babies?"

Krista's anger has subsided. She lowers her head and tears stream down her face.

"I was pregnant eighteen months ago. My boyfriend and I wanted to get married, but my parents wouldn't discuss anything except an abortion. My mom and dad went on and on about how my mom had gotten pregnant when they were dating and they got married because of the pregnancies. They kept saying over and over again how having to get married had ruined their lives. When my mom took me to a clinic to schedule an abortion, they told me I was going to have twins. My mom still wouldn't listen. My mom and dad told me they would never speak to me again or have anything to do with me if I had the babies. I had the abortion. I hate my mom and dad. I hate God for not letting me keep my babies. I stay high as much as I can so that I don't have to remember the abortion."

Alyssa recognizes that what she has seen as defiant behavior has actually been Krista's attempts to cope with grief about the abortion. Alyssa quickly recognizes that Krista will need support and guidance to cope with her grief.

Approximately one in three pregnancies end in abortion.[4] Therefore, it shouldn't be surprising that we have teens in our youth groups struggling to cope with previous abortions or making choices to have abortions. What may be most difficult for us to acknowledge is that we have parents in our churches who see abortion as the best, or the only way, to deal with teen pregnancy. Parents who may not view abortion as an option for other teens may quickly change their mind about abortion when their own daughters are pregnant. An abortion is a short-term convenient solution to a difficult problem. With an abortion, teens don't have to deal with the emotional and physical consequences of pregnancy. They don't have to choose adoptive parents or raise a child as a single parent. Most importantly for many parents, the pregnant teen doesn't have to maintain a relationship with the father of the child or include the father of the child in decisions being made about the child. However, we must help parents and teens recognize that an abortion has serious, negative spiritual consequences.

Coping with Abortion

If a teen is considering an abortion, it is important to explore the reasons for choosing an abortion. If the teen is choosing an abortion to avoid telling her parents about a pregnancy, it is important to discuss long-term spiritual consequences of the decision. Again, don't discount the possibility that the teen may have parents who are encouraging an abortion because it is convenient. Be aware of your state laws regarding abortion and the rights of the parents of the pregnant teen in making decisions in regards to an abortion. If at all possible, you should try to get the teen to talk to a trained mental health professional if she is considering an abortion. A trained mental health professional will be more capable of providing relevant information and assistance.

Similarly, if you are dealing with a teen who has had an abortion, you can provide support and help the teen recognize the forgiving nature of God. However, if the teen is having significant difficulty coping with the abortion, she will need the assistance of a trained mental health professional.

Sexually Transmitted Diseases

Teens will be diagnosed with sexually transmitted diseases (STDs) in large numbers. However, I've deliberately chosen not to emphasize STDs in this book for the following reasons:

- Diagnosing STDs should be left to medical professionals
- Teens tell me that adults emphasize STDs and pregnancy too much in discussions about sexuality
- Types of prevalent STDs changes too rapidly for this book to be an accurate resource
- There is an abundance of available, up-to-date sources to provide information on STDs
- Teens probably won't approach youth workers with concerns about STDs because there are many community health resources available to deal with STDs.

If teens do approach you with concerns about STDs, I recommend that you make a referral to a community health clinic or contact the health clinic and get information for teens. (If you need more information concerning the symptoms, causes, and treatments for STDs, the American Social Health Association provides up-to-date medical information on its Web site at www.ashastd.org.)

The Challenge

Pregnancy provides a unique opportunity in a youth group. Dealing with a teen who is pregnant provides us with a chance to demonstrate Christian compassion and forgiveness. Yet we have some responsibility to provide spiritual guidance to help teens acknowledge their wrongdoing. We should expect a similar acknowledgment of wrongdoing concerning any sexual behavior outside a marriage relationship. However, with teen pregnancy, we are modeling publicly for our teens how to balance forgiveness with accountability. We must earnestly seek God's guidance in dealing with pregnant teens as we balance forgiveness with accountability.

A particular area of caution in dealing with pregnant teens is making sure that we don't become overly involved in the family situation. Unlike many of the other sexual issues discussed in this book, teens cannot hide pregnancy from their parents (unless they have an abortion). Frequently, the initial shock of pregnancy may be difficult for the teen's parents to handle. However, if we become too involved in the family dynamics, we may prevent the parents and their teen from working through the situation. Conflict is necessary at times to help families confront issues and develop more healthy ways of interacting. If a family is having significant difficulties dealing with pregnancy after the initial shock, we need to involve mental health professionals rather than becoming overly involved in the family dynamics ourselves.

RESPONDING TO THE CHALLENGE

1. What are some reasons why a teen in your youth group might intentionally get pregnant?

_____

_____

_____

_____

2. If a teen is pregnant, but has not had intercourse, what might have occurred?

_____

_____

_____

_____

3. What do some teens believe about pregnancy and oral sex?

_____

_____

_____

_____

4. How do we provide encouragement and support for pregnant teens without endorsing premarital sex?

_____

_____

_____

_____

If we don't acknowledge the
influence of media and address
it with members of our youth groups,
we are silently endorsing media
as the teacher of Sex Ed 101.
When we don't provide information
about sexuality to our teens,
the media will.

8
Dating Violence

When Ken picks Julie up at her house, she is nervous. She's fourteen years old and Ken, who is sixteen, has invited her to a party at his parents' house. Tonight is the first time Julie's parents have let her go on a date with a guy old enough to drive his own car. One of the reasons her parents let her go on a date with Ken is that Ken is a leader in the youth group and his parents will be at home to supervise the party.

During the party, Julie is flattered by all the attention Ken is giving her. He laughs at her jokes and keeps his arm around her shoulder when they are sitting on the couch. Most of the kids are playing different card games in the living room and den. Eventually, Ken asks Julie if she wants to see his room. She shrugs and smiles. She doesn't feel uncomfortable going to Ken's room because his parents are supervising the party and there are lots of other kids in the house. Ken takes Julie's hand as they walk down the hall to his room. He opens the door to his room and let's Julie walk into the room ahead of him. After he walks into the room, he closes the door behind him and pulls Julie toward him. He kisses her tentatively at first, then more forcefully. Julie is caught off guard and tries to back away from Ken.

As Julie stumbles backward, Ken pushes toward her. She backs into the bed and Ken forces her down. Julie panics and lunges for the side of the bed. Ken anticipates her movement and pins her to the bed. Ken puts a forearm across her throat, while he uses his other hand to pull up her dress. He rips her panties off and unzips his trousers.

Julie is gasping for air. Ken's arm is cutting off her oxygen. Julie realizes that Ken is going to rape her. She wants to scream, but she can't. She can't stop Ken as he straddles her and rapes her. His weight shifts, but she still can't catch her breath. Ken rolls off the bed, tucks his shirt in, and zips his pants. Julie is sprawled across the bed with her dress pulled up. Tears roll down her cheeks as she struggles to breathe.

"Get up. We can't stay in here all night," commands Ken.

Julie gets up off the bed and tugs her dress down.

"Clean your face up. Don't cry about this. You wanted it just like I did."

Julie doesn't reply as she wipes her face. Julie's body shakes as Ken reaches over and says, "Don't you dare tell anyone about this. No one will believe you. If you tell anyone about this, I'll tell them that you came on to me and wanted it. If anyone believes you, they will just think you are a slut."

Although it seems like an eternity to Julie, they have been in Ken's bedroom less than ten minutes. As they walk out of Ken's bedroom, Ken grabs her hand again and says, "Smile." Julie smiles as they walk back into the living room. Ken continues to act like nothing has happened.

Julie is representative of teens who will experience date rape. Acquaintance rape and date rape represent 70% to 80% of rape crisis center cases.[1] Over half of the teenage females who are raped are raped by a date.[2] Of the teens who are raped, 78% never tell their parents, while 70% will tell a friend about the rape.[3] Three out of four females who have sex before they are fourteen indicate they were forced to have sex.[4] The younger a female is, the more likely it is that she was forced to have sex.[5]

In Julie's case, she doesn't immediately tell anyone about the rape because she believes that she is to blame for the date rape. However, she eventually tells a friend in her youth group about the incident during a week at church camp. Julie's friend talks with a youth worker.

Recognizing the Symptoms

The symptoms of date rape, like the symptoms of other types of sexual trauma, may vary greatly. If the teen has not experienced any other type of sexual trauma prior to the date rape, there may be significant behavioral changes. If the teen has been outgoing and involved in several peer activities, she may become much quieter and less interested in social activities. There may also be changes in the dating relationship of the teen. The teen may cut off a relationship with the perpetrator or may continue to see the perpetrator, but the relationship will appear to be dominated by the perpetrator. Likewise, the teen may experience difficulties sleeping or have nightmares. In addition, the teen may withdraw from church activities and may be less willing to engage in typical family activities. Remember that symptoms of date rape will vary greatly from one teen to another and that these symptoms may also indicate other issues.

Myths Promoting Sexual Violence

Male Myths	Female Myths
■ Teenage females want sex, but don't think it is okay to admit it. How they dress tells us they want sex.	■ I'm not the type of female who gets raped. That only happens to women who don't date "good" guys.
■ Teenage females want guys to take charge of sexual situations, so they won't feel like what they are doing is wrong.	■ Teenage males have raging hormones and can't control their sex drives. It's my fault if he gets turned on.
■ Women won't say this, but they all like rough sex.	■ He cares about me. It won't hurt to give in a little bit to show him I love him.
■ It won't hurt for us to drink a few drinks or for me to slip a little something in a drink to help her relax. She wants to have sex, she's just nervous.	■ He wouldn't get me drunk or give me drugs to get me to have sex with him. He's not that kind of guy.
■ When I spend my time or money on a date, she owes me something.	■ If he spends his time or money on me, I owe him something.

Physical Violence

Melissa and John started dating about a month ago. Melissa is active in the youth group and enjoys interacting with other kids in the youth group. Melissa has convinced John to start attending youth group activities with her. One evening after the youth group activity is over, Melissa talks with several of the guys in the youth group. When John sees Melissa talking with the other guys, he becomes enraged. He assumes she is flirting with the guys and hurries over to the group. He grabs Melissa by the arm and yanks her away from the other teens.

"It's time for us to go," he hisses through clenched teeth.

"I'm not finished talking yet."

"Yes, you are. We are leaving."

When they get to the car, John is still angry.

"I can't believe you are flirting with those guys right in front of me. What kind of slut are you? Can't you be happy with one guy? Are you trying to embarrass me in front of everyone?"

Melissa tries to explain that she has known the guys in the

youth group for years and they are more like brothers to her. John doesn't listen. He continues to call her a slut and accuse her of flirting with the other guys. When they reach Melissa's house, John tells Melissa to get out of the car before he hits her. Melissa is scared and scrambles out of the car in a panic.

The next morning, Melissa's arm is bruised where John grabbed it to drag her away from the group. Melissa is upset and thinks that she must have done something to provoke John. She begins to believe that maybe talking with the guys in the youth group isn't appropriate.

That evening when John sees Melissa, he brings her roses and apologizes for his behavior and promises that he won't ever do anything to hurt her again. Melissa believes John and continues to date him, but the violence and the apologies continue. Melissa continues to believe if she changes her own behavior enough, John won't hit her.

Melissa remains in her dating relationship with John and eventually marries him. The physical assaults continue and escalate when they get married. Melissa is like the approximately one in three teens experiencing violence in dating relationships.[6] Interestingly, of the men and women involved in violent dating relationships, nearly a third of the men and women thought abuse signified love and that the relationship improved after violent episodes.[7] Dealing with violent dating relationships involves the unique challenge of dispelling myths about violent relationships.

Characteristics of Abusers

Teens engaging in violent behavior may have the following characteristics:
- A volatile temper
- Incidents of pushing, kicking, or hitting others when angry
- Breaks things or throws things when angry
- Jealous of others and spies on boyfriend/girlfriend
- Tells boyfriend/girlfriend how to dress
- Picks friends and makes decisions for girlfriend/boyfriend
- Uses guilt to manipulate boyfriend/girlfriend
- Threatens to harm self or others to control girlfriend/boyfriend

Myths Promoting Physical Violence

Myth	Reality
Jealousy is a sign of love.	Jealousy is a sign that someone is controlling and possessive, not that someone loves you.
When a woman gets hit by a date, she must have provoked him in some way.	Even if someone is provoked and feels angry, violence is always wrong. Frequently, women do not provoke the violence.
Women in abusive dating relationships stay because they enjoy being abused.	Most women stay in an abusive relationship because they want to improve the relationship rather than ending it. Teens may feel particular pressure to stay because having a "bad" boyfriend is better than having no boyfriend.
Maybe things will get better.	Once violence begins in a dating relationship, it usually gets worse. The only way to stop the violence is to end the relationship or to get counseling to break the pattern.
I can tell if a guy is going to be a "hitter" just by looking at him.	Abusers come from all racial, ethnic, cultural, socio-economic, and religious groups.
It will never happen to me!	Dating violence can happen to you. Everyone is at risk.

Adapted from National Clearinghouse on Family Violence. Dating Violence. Available at: www.hc-sc.gc.ca/hppb/familyviolence/html/datingeng.html.

Sexual Harassment

Karen used to enjoy youth group activities, now she dreads them. She tries to convince her parents not to make her go to the activities, but they ground her when she doesn't go to scheduled youth group activities. Lately, she has decided on some occasions that she would rather be grounded than to experience the harassment that happens in youth group activities.

Several months ago, one of the guys in the youth group asked her, "Karen, do you want to suck my dick?" All the other guys who heard the comment began laughing. Karen was embarrassed and her face turned a deep shade of red. Karen turned away from the group and joined some of the other girls in the youth group. The guys continued to point at her and laugh for the rest of the evening, but Karen assumed that when the evening was over, the teasing would end.

During the next youth group activity, a different guy came up behind Karen and pinched her bottom and pushed his groin against her. "You been thinking about me?" he asked. Again the same guys pointed at her and laughed during the rest of the activity.

The same pattern continued at every youth activity. After a couple of weeks of guys making all kinds of sexual suggestions, Karen told her parents that the guys in the youth group were teasing her. She didn't tell them specifically about the sexual comments because she was embarrassed. Her parents told her to ignore the comments and eventually the teasing would stop. The sexual comments didn't stop.

Karen began to withdraw from the other teens in the youth group. Several of the other girls in the youth group tried to get the guys to leave her alone, but the guys continued to make sexual comments and suggestions to her. Karen tried talking to youth workers, but again she didn't tell them about the specific comments.

Finally, one of Karen's friends went to talk with the youth minister. The youth minister was stunned at the behavior. He had recognized that some of the guys had been teasing Karen, but he had not recognized that the teasing was sexual. The youth minister called the parents of the guys and asked them to come to a meeting. The youth minister explained to the parents what had been occurring in the youth activities. The sexual harassment ended immediately and all of the guys apologized for their behavior. They hadn't realized how inappropriate and damaging their remarks were.

Karen is representative of the 83% of female and 60% of male teens experiencing sexual harassment.[8] Sexual harassment is sexual behavior that is unwanted, not liked, unwelcomed, and occurs on a frequent basis. It generally occurs in public places and often with adult witnesses, particularly at school. The target is likely to feel frustrated, nervous, isolated, and demeaned.

Keep in mind that the church is liable for sexual harassment occurring in youth group activities if adults know about the harassment or reasonably should have known or if there have been complaints about harassment and the church fails to take immediate and appropriate steps to remedy the situation.

	Sexual Harassment
Physical Contact	Grabbing, touching, or pinching in a sexual manner, pulling clothes down or off, blocking or cornering someone in a threatening way
Verbal Contact	Sexual taunting or teasing, sexual jokes, rumors, sexual references
Social Contact	Obscene gestures, repeated pressure for dates, sexual advances or propositions that are not wanted, telephone calls, notes, letters, or e-mails that come repeatedly despite the fact that the sender has been rebuffed

Why Teens Sexually Harass Others

- Teens think it is funny.
- Teens don't know it's inappropriate.
- Teens don't recognize it is offensive.
- Peers model harassing behaviors.
- Everyone is doing it.
- Teens want to fit in with their peers.
- Teens don't want their peers to harass them.[9]

Why Teens Don't Leave Abusive Relationships

- **Teens believe it is their fault.** Teens perpetrating violence often blame their victims. The victims begin to believe it is their fault. The victims believe that if they were able to behave differently or do some tasks perfectly, the violence would stop.
- **Teens aren't sure that it is rape.** Teens may believe that they did not clearly communicate to their date that they did not want to have sex, or they may believe that their date is entitled to have sex with them because the date paid for a meal or a movie.

■ **Teens care about the perpetrator.** Teens genuinely believe that they love the violent perpetrator. They don't want to get the perpetrator in trouble and they don't want to hurt the perpetrator's feelings.

■ **Teens believe that the perpetrator will change.** Teens believe that if they change their behavior, the perpetrator will change. Frequently, perpetrators of physical violence will be repentant after the assault. The perpetrator will promise to change.

■ **Teens don't want to upset the perpetrator.** Teens may not want to report the physical abuse because they don't want to upset the perpetrator. They may fear retaliation from the perpetrator.

■ **Teens believe their relationships are normal.** Teens don't have much experience with dating and may believe that all dating relationships have elements of physical violence. Similarly, teens may not report sexually harassing behavior because it is so widely accepted among their peers.

■ **Teens don't want the relationship to end.** If teens recognize physical aggression is inappropriate, they may not report the assaults because they don't want their parents to tell them to end the relationship.

■ **Teens don't know where to get help.** Since we don't frequently discuss violent dating relationships, teens don't know what adults or agencies are available to help them deal with dating violence.

■ **Teens fear that other people won't believe them.** As with other types of violent situations, teens may feel like other people won't believe them. Perhaps the persons they are dating are popular at school or in the youth group.

■ **Teens are embarrassed to admit what has happened.** In situations involving dating violence, teens are frequently humiliated and degraded by sexual harassment, sexual assault, or physical assault. Because these experiences have been so degrading, teens may be embarrassed to report what has happened.

Knowing What to Do

■ **Don't promise confidentiality.** In many states, if teens tell you they have been raped, you will be legally required to report the rape. Don't promise teens you won't tell anyone what they say to you. Explain the limits of confidentiality to them. Generally, they will still tell you about the abuse.

■ **Believe the story.** As a general rule, teens do not make up stories about being raped. You need to assume the story is true. You don't have the skills to determine if a teen is making up an accusation.

- **Let teens know they don't deserve abuse.** If teens have been in violent dating relationships for an extended period of time, they may believe that they deserve the physical and sexual abuse. While these teens may have low self-esteem, it is critical that they recognize that there is never any reason for violence to occur.

- **Don't be critical of the abusing date.** While it is an immediate and normal reaction for us to be critical of the abuser, it is important to remember that the victim cares about the abuser. Being critical of the abuser may only alienate the victim.

- **Don't ask blaming questions.** Questions like "What did you do to provoke him?" or "Why don't you just break up with him?" may make teens think you are blaming them.

- **Assure teens it is not their fault.** If a peer forces a teen to engage in sexual acts against their will, the perpetrator is responsible. Teens who pay for meals or movies on dates are not entitled to sexual favors as payment. Although teens may make poor decisions allowing perpetrators to isolate them in a secluded location, the sexual assault is still not their fault.

- **Develop a safety plan.** If a teen reports rape or date rape to you, you must make sure that the accused perpetrator does not have access to the teen. Make sure that the teen is safe from verbal harassment, sexual harassment, and physical threats.

- **Notify authorities.** You need to be aware of your state laws concerning rape, physical assault, and sexual harassment. If teens are involved in violent dating relationships, you may have to report information to the police or child protective services. In most states if the teen is under 17 years of age, you are legally required to report any non-consensual sex to police. In fact, in many states if the teen consents to sex with someone over eighteen, it is still illegal and has to be reported to authorities. Because the teen is a minor, you may also be required to report physical assaults and/or sexual harassment.

- **Notify parents.** If you are required to report a dating incident to the police, it is generally a good idea to help teens notify their parents about the situation. In some cases, teens may not have the right to keep information confidential from their parents. Teens may not want to tell their parents about dating violence, but generally parents are supportive of teens.

In Over Your Head

As you consider what to do to help teens deal with dating violence, recognize that there will be situations when you need to refer teens for professional counseling services to help them deal with dating violence. If the answer to any of the following questions is yes, then you may need to refer the teen to a professional counselor.

- Is the teen having significant difficulty with dating relationships?
- Is the teen continuing to withdraw from peers?
- Is the teen continuing to withdraw from social activities?
- Is the teen having significant behavioral problems?
- Did the dating violence occur for a long period of time?
- Did the parents or other adults refuse to believe the teen?
- Did the violence continue after the teen reported it?
- Did the abuser retaliate when the teen reported?
- Is the teen expected to participate in court proceedings?

A Word of Caution

Most of the information in this chapter has been directed toward helping the victims of dating violence, not the perpetrators of dating violence. While perpetrators of dating violence need our spiritual guidance and support, they generally need the assistance of trained professionals to address the issues of dating violence. Help the perpetrators find competent mental health professionals who can help them address their anger management and physical aggression. Refusing to make a referral to a mental health provider may only perpetuate the cycle.

The Challenge

Dating violence is particularly challenging for youth workers because victimized teens lose confidence in their ability to make good decisions. They believe they should have recognized that perpetrators were violent and they don't trust their ability to choose friends or dates. Likewise, teens blame themselves for being alone with perpetrators in secluded places. Frequently they blame themselves for date rapes because they believe they did not clearly communicate they weren't interested in sex.

From a spiritual perspective, dating violence may cause teens to question how God could allow them to be hurt and may be angry with

God. Teens may struggle with their feelings of guilt and their feelings that they are "dirty" and can't have a relationship with God. Youth workers have the unique challenge of gently encouraging teens to forgive themselves and to recognize that God isn't responsible for dating violence.

RESPONDING TO THE CHALLENGE

1. What myths contribute to date rape?

_____

_____

_____

_____

2. Teens may believe that being physically violent in a dating relationship is acceptable. What myths about dating violence contribute to this belief?

_____

_____

_____

_____

3. What are some characteristics of teens who are likely to be violent in a dating relationship?

_____

_____

_____

_____

4. If a teen is being abused in a relationship, what symptoms will we see?

_____

_____

_____

_____

5. What types of behaviors are forms of sexual harassment?

_____

_____

_____

_____

6. Why do teens sexually harass others?

_____

_____

_____

_____

7. If teens are in an abusive relationship, why don't they leave the relationship?

_____

_____

_____

_____

9

Sexual Abuse

During Maria's eighth-grade year, her parents befriend her softball coach, Jaclyn, because Jaclyn's mother is diagnosed with cancer. Maria's mother becomes the primary emotional support for Jaclyn as she deals with her mother's deteriorating health. In turn, Maria mirrors her mother's efforts to provide comfort and support for her softball coach. She sends cards and Bible verses to encourage Jaclyn.

When Jaclyn's mother dies, she begins to talk to Maria more about her mother and her own grief. Gradually, Maria becomes Jaclyn's primary emotional support. Although Maria's parents are concerned about Maria assuming a peer relationship with her coach, they are good friends with Jaclyn and expect that as Jaclyn resolves her grief that the relationship will taper off. Even though the relationship continues to be emotionally intense, Maria's parents reassure themselves that Jaclyn is a coach at a Christian school and is a good Christian. As much as they are concerned about Maria's overwhelming concern for Jaclyn, they allow the relationship to continue.

One weekend, Maria's mother attends a ladies retreat sponsored by her church. Jaclyn calls Maria after the other women have left for the retreat and tells Maria she wants to attend the retreat and asks Maria to ride with her to the retreat. Maria agrees. When Jaclyn and Maria get to the retreat area, they have to share a room because there aren't other rooms available. They sit up for several hours talking about Jaclyn's grief.

In the early morning hours, they go to bed. Some time later, Maria awakes when she feel's Jaclyn's hands caressing her breasts. Maria's body stiffens, but she keeps her eyes closed hoping that Jaclyn will think that she is asleep. Maria can't believe what is happening. Surely Jaclyn is asleep. Jaclyn wouldn't do this to her. Eventually Jaclyn's hands stop. Maria lies awake staring at the ceiling after Jaclyn's steady breathing indicates she is asleep.

The next morning when Maria gets up, she doesn't mention the incident and pretends it didn't happen. Jaclyn never mentions the situation. Both Jaclyn and Maria spend the day in Bible study together with the other women on the retreat. That night, they both go back to their room and talk about the day's lessons. They both go to bed without mentioning the previous night's incident. Although Maria is anxious, she believes the previous night's incident was a mistake or that maybe she was dreaming. Eventually she falls asleep.

Again, Jaclyn's hands awaken her. Maria pretends she is asleep. Nothing is said about what happens the next morning. Maria thinks about telling her mother, but what would her mother think about Jaclyn? Would Jaclyn get in trouble? Her mom might not let her see Jaclyn anymore, and Jaclyn needs her help to cope with her mother's death.

That weekend becomes the beginning of nearly five years of sexual interactions between Jaclyn and Maria. Eventually Maria can't pretend she is asleep any longer because of the invasiveness of Jaclyn's sexual activities. When Maria graduates from high school, she knows that she needs to get away from Jaclyn to end the relationship. Maria chooses to attend college two thousand miles away from home to break off the relationship with Jaclyn.

I met Maria eighteen months after she broke off the relationship with Jaclyn. She struggled with feeling guilt about the sexual relationship and feeling responsible for Jaclyn's emotional health. Maria was actively involved in church activities, as she had been all the way through high school. From the outside, everything looked great in Maria's life, but from the inside she was hiding a terrible secret.

Maria is one of 1.3 million children a year that are sexually abused.[1] Approximately one in three women and one in six men are sexually abused before age 18,[2] and an estimated 61 percent of sexual assault victims are under the age of 18.[3] With such a large number of children and teens being sexually abused, youth workers need to recognize the symptoms of abuse and need to know how to respond to sexual abuse situations.

Recognizing the Symptoms

Recognizing the symptoms of sexual abuse can be difficult. If teens have been repeatedly sexually abused since childhood, there may not be noticeable changes in their behavior during adolescence. However, if an abusive sexual relationship begins during adolescence, there may be marked changes in a teen's behavior.

Symptoms of Sexual Abuse	
Physical Symptoms	Insomnia, headaches, stomachaches, vomiting, nausea, pregnancy, or sexually transmitted diseases
Sexual Symptoms	Wearing seductive clothing, engaging in seductive posturing, removing clothing in inappropriate situations, openly asking for sex, having sex with multiple partners, engaging in prostitution or sexually aggressive behaviors, masturbating frequently or in public, or developing an aversion to anything sexual
Emotional Symptoms	Depression, anger, anxiety, sudden mood changes, crying easily or frequently, being irritable, making negative statements about one's self
Behavioral Symptoms	Changes in sleeping or eating habits, poor hygiene, lack of concern about appearance, wearing loose fitting clothing, changes in school grades or performance in class, withdrawal from family or friends, refusing to comply with adult requests, or being overly compliant with adult requests
Delinquent Symptoms	Drug or alcohol use, running away, truancy, aggressiveness and bullying

One of the difficulties in discussing the symptoms of sexual abuse is that different teens may exhibit different symptoms when they are sexually abused. In addition, some of these same symptoms may indicate other issues in teens' lives. However, the emergence of several of these symptoms, particularly sexual symptoms, should raise concerns among youth workers.

Why Teens Don't Report

Even though teens recognize that sexual interactions with adults are wrong, they frequently do not report inappropriate sexual contact with adults. Teens hesitate to report sexual contact with adults for several reasons.

■ **Teens think no one will believe them.** Sexual offenders tell teens no one will believe them. Frequently, the sexual offender is a highly respected member of the church community who might be believed instead of the child.

■ **Teens genuinely care about the sexual perpetrator and don't want the perpetrator punished.** Remember, the sexual offender may be a close family friend, and frequently establishes an emotional relationship with the teen before engaging in sexual activity.

■ **Teens feel tremendous guilt about the sexual behavior and don't want other people to know about it.** A teen may feel soiled physically, emotionally, and spiritually by having sexual contact with an adult. As a result, teens have a sense of unworthiness and blame themselves for the sexual contact with an adult.

■ **Teens may see the sexual relationship with the adult as romantic and want the sexual contact to continue.** Whatever the teen's feelings about the relationship, it is important for adults to clearly distinguish between the role of an adult and that of a child in this situation. The adult is always at fault, both legally and morally, for initiating a sexual relationship with a minor.

■ **Teens don't know where to get help.** Although teens may want help, they often don't know what adults they can trust. Similarly, they don't know if adults are capable of dealing with the disclosure. Teens are often extremely hesitant to tell their parents because they are afraid of how their parents will react. If teens don't know if an adult will be capable of helping them deal with sexual abuse, they may drop hints about the perpetrator or they may try to "get caught."

Internet Issues

Christina, a thirteen-year-old, lives with her aunt and attends a private religious school. Since moving in with her aunt two years ago, Christina has become involved in studying religious materials. She is actively involved in cheerleading at school, a good student, and an altar girl at church. She tries to make kids laugh and smile when she interacts with them in her neighborhood. She is spirited and outgoing with her friends.

Without her aunt's knowledge, Christina lives out a different life on the Internet. In contrast to how she interacts at school, she develops her own Web site entitled "sxyme4utosee." Christina has a dozen provocative screen names in chat rooms. She engages in interactions on the Internet involving sexual dialogue. As part of her interactions on the Internet, Christina arranges to meet men for sexual encounters.

One evening, Christina's aunt drops Christina off to meet her friends at the mall, but Christina is actually planning to meet a 25-year-old man to have sex. She's not concerned about the encounter because she has met this man and other men for similar sexual encounters. This time, something goes wrong. Christina never returns home. Police eventually find her body and determine that she was strangled by the man she met to have sex.

Christina Long, who was killed in the summer of 2002, demonstrates how the Internet allows pedophiles and sexual predators to have immediate access to potential victims. Through the Internet, a sexual predator can assume any identity to approach teens, including pretending to be a teen himself. Frequently, these assumed identities are elaborate with the sexual predator providing pictures of a teen male and identifying the pictures as being him. A sexual predator can also enter teen chat rooms to learn personal information about potential victims and then develop an online relationship with a teen.

The sexual predator may spend months establishing a relationship with a teen so that the teen will trust him. Don't underestimate the planning and patience that sexual predators can have in pursuing their victims. Eventually, the sexual predator will manipulate the situation to set up a meeting with his victim. If the sexual predator is unable to manipulate the teen to schedule a voluntary meeting, he may use the Internet to track down the home address of the potential victim and then monitor her activities until he finds an opportunity to molest her.

Recognizing the Risks

■ **Anonymity.** Part of the allure of initiating relationships in chat rooms and through instant messenger technology is the ability to be anonymous. The price for accepting anonymity on the Internet is that being able to remain anonymous frequently removes inhibitions. When someone can remain anonymous, he or she is much more willing to engage in inappropriate or risky behaviors.

■ **Access.** The Internet gives sexual predators instant access to thousands of potential victims. In addition to being able to access victims through chat rooms and instant messaging technology, predators can obtain addresses and other information for potential victims.

■ **Acceptance.** Using the Internet as a way to communicate and establish relationships is becoming widely accepted in our society. Parents and other adults don't view the Internet as threatening because they don't recognize that people accessing teens on the Internet may present a physical or sexual threat to a teen.

■ **Different rules.** Through the Internet, teens frequently share personal information and develop relationships with anonymous individuals. Interestingly, parents and adults generally wouldn't allow teens to engage in the same level of disclosure and emotional intimacy in a personal face-to-face relationship without some level of screening. Most parents want to meet their children's friends and know about social activities, yet parents don't provide the same level of supervision on the Internet.

Internet Safety

Dealing with sexuality on the Internet will require that both teens and parents be aware of the risks of the Internet and the following safety precautions.

■ **Monitor computer access.** Teens who are using a computer should have an adult in the room. Adults should frequently check what teens are doing on the Internet. Adults should monitor contact while teens are on the Internet, but they should also check the history of the sites teens are accessing.

■ **Use a filter.** Parents can have filter installed on a computer to prevent teens from accessing Web sites that have pornographic material or other objectionable content.

■ **Protect your identity.** Don't give out your name, your address, or other personal information on the Internet. For teens, don't identify where you go to high school, where you work, or where you go to church. Similarly, don't give out information about your gender or age.

■ **Strangers not allowed.** Only interact with people you know through e-mail, instant messenger, and chat rooms. Don't use the Internet to develop relationships with strangers. For teens, the dangers far outweigh the benefits because teens don't have the skills to determine who is appropriate and inappropriate on the Internet.

Incest

Frequently, churches have the most difficulty dealing with sexual abuse incidents that involve family members. When the perpetrator is a member of the teen's family, the family often struggles to reconcile the issues. In fact, teens who experience incest are often not believed by their own family members. If teens experience a great deal of resistance to an outcry of sexual abuse involving a family member, they will often change their stories and deny that any abuse occurred. Parents will often refuse to believe that one sibling is sexually abusing another sibling or that their spouses are abusing their children. Churches have difficulty believing allegations against church leaders or respected members of the community. Keep in mind that sexual perpetrators come from all racial, ethnic, socio-economic, and religious groups. Even a church leader may be a perpetrator.

Incest is a particularly difficult sexual abuse situation that requires professional mental health services for the family. The word of caution for youth ministry workers is teens seldom make outcries of sexual abuse if it is not occurring. If a teen is making a false allegation, let the professional law enforcement and mental health providers make that determination. Remember that your job is to minister to teens. While the extended family needs significant help, your focus should be to support the teen.

Knowing What to Do

■ **Don't promise confidentiality.** In many states, if a teen tells you that she is engaged in a sexual relationship with an adult, you will have to report the situation to authorities. Don't promise teens you won't tell anyone what they say to you. Explain the limits of confidentiality to them. Generally, they will still tell you about the abuse.

■ **Believe the story.** As a general rule, teens do not make up stories about being sexually abused. You need to assume the story is true. You don't have the skills to determine if a teen is making up an accusation.

■ **Assure teens it is not their fault.** An adult is always responsible for initiating a sexual relationship with a teen. Even if a teen tries to initiate a sexual relationship with an adult, it is the adult's job to maintain an appropriate physical and sexual relationship with a teen.

■ **Develop a safety plan.** Immediately develop a plan to keep the teen away from the perpetrator. If the perpetrator has access to the teen through church activities, then the perpetrator and the teen do

---

not need to be at the same events or activities.

- **Notify authorities.** You need to be aware of your state laws concerning child abuse. In most states, if the teen is under 17 years of age, you are legally required to report any suspected abuse to the police or a child protection agency.
- **Obtain medical help.** If a sexual assault has just occurred, you need to take the teen to a rape crisis center or emergency room for medical care. You should notify parents and ask them to meet you at the medical facility.
- **Notify parents.** In most states, teens do not have a right to keep information about sexual abuse confidential from their parents. Teens may not want to talk with their parents, but in my experience, parents are usually amazingly resilient and supportive in helping their teens deal with sexual abuse. An obvious exception to notifying parents is if a parent or sibling is the perpetrator. If a family member is the perpetrator, allow the police or child protective services to notify the family.

In Over Your Head

As you consider what to do to help teens deal with sexual abuse, recognize that there will be situations when you need to refer teens for professional counseling services to help them deal with sexual abuse. If the answer to any of the following questions is yes, then you may need to refer the teen to a professional counselor.

- Is the teen having significant behavioral problems?
- Was the sexual abuse repeated for a long period of time?
- Did more than one perpetrator abuse the teen?
- Did the sexual abuse also involve physical violence?
- Did adults refuse to believe the teen when the abuse was reported?
- Is the teen going to have to participate in court proceedings?
- Is the perpetrator a member of the family?

The Challenge

The challenge for youth workers in responding to sexual abuse is to help teens access the appropriate resources initially. Frequently, teens and their families will need assistance in accessing counseling services and in dealing with the legal system. Youth workers can provide support and encouragement for the teen and the family in the initial response to sexual violence.

Ultimately, the teen will need help in learning to trust people again. Similarly, teens may need help in dealing with feelings of guilt and confusion about sexual issues. Teens may even try to protect their parents from dealing with the emotional responses of learning a teen has been abused. Youth workers who are addressing sexual issues in Bible classes or devotionals need to recognize that as many as one in three of the females and one in six of the males listening to the lesson may have been sexually abused.

RESPONDING TO THE CHALLENGE

1. If a teen is being sexually abused, what symptoms could we see?

2. Why don't teens report incidents of sexual abuse?

3. How does the Internet provide opportunities for sexual predators?

4. What are some precautions teens should take when using the Internet?

5. If teens have been sexually abused, what should we do to help them?

While our culture promotes dating
as an opportunity to experiment
sexually and to engage in
sexual relationships with
multiple partners, the Bible
calls us to engage in
sexual relationships only
in the context of a marriage.
We must teach teens that dating
is an opportunity for personal growth
and exploration unrelated
to sexual activities.

10

Homosexuality

Betty volunteers with the youth ministry program at her church. She has worked with teens for nearly five years and enjoys it immensely. She is married with no children and seems to connect exceptionally well with teens. Betty is an anomaly among youth workers because she is comfortable talking about dating and sexuality with teens.

Despite Betty's ease in discussing sexuality with teens she's not prepared for her conversation with Suzie, a parent. Suzie calls Betty at home and schedules a time to meet with her after Bible study one evening. After some initial discussion about youth group activities, the following conversation takes place.

"Betty, I'm concerned about my daughter, Jennifer. She has been good friends with Heather since they started elementary school together. Heather has practically lived at our house for several years when Jennifer isn't living at her house. They have been inseparable for years.

"Recently, Jennifer confided in me. She told me that Heather believes she is a lesbian. Heather has been hanging out with different friends at school. These new friends are labeled as homosexual by the other teens. Jennifer is concerned about Heather, but she doesn't want to change her relationship with Heather.

"I'm worried. Jennifer says she isn't interested in Heather in a sexual way, but I'm concerned that Jennifer will be labeled as a lesbian by other kids and will be harassed. What am I supposed to do? Do I continue to let Jennifer and Heather hang out together? Do I change how much I let Jennifer see Heather? I don't know what to do."

Betty doesn't know what to tell Suzie, but she tells Suzie that she will think about the situation and come up with some ideas. They agree to meet again in a week and close their discussion with a prayer.

One of the greatest cultural changes that teens face is the openness and acceptance of homosexuality. Teens are becoming more accepting of homosexuality with gay and lesbian youth alliances being formed in public schools to help teens explore their sexual identities and to affirm their sexual orientation. Teens encounter gay and lesbian peers who are holding hands in the school hallways or who are escorting each other to school proms.

Television programs depict homosexual lifestyles as an acceptable alternative lifestyle. Homosexual characters are seen engaging in sexual acts and as maintaining healthy relationships with their partners. Similarly, teens are exposed to music that endorses homosexuality.

In contrast to the messages presented in the media, teens may still see peers who are homosexual being taunted and ridiculed. While there are schools where teens identifying themselves as homosexual can attend a prom together, there are also schools where teens identified as homosexual are shunned by their peers. Teens may hear their Christian friends making jokes, callous remarks, and cruel comments about homosexuality. These mixed messages leave teens confused about homosexuality. In the midst of this confusion are teens who are struggling with concerns about homosexuality.

What's Does It Mean?

- **Homosexual:** Being sexually and emotionally attracted to a person of the same sex.
- **Heterosexual:** Being sexually and emotionally attracted to a person of the opposite sex.
- **Bisexual:** Being sexually and emotionally attracted to people of the same sex and the opposite sex.
- **Sexual Orientation:** A person's preference for homosexual, heterosexual, or bisexual behavior.
- **Gender role:** The culturally expected behaviors for men and women. For instance, a woman who is a car mechanic is not abiding by an expected gender role.

Homosexual Friends

In the opening scenario of the chapter, Suzie raises a legitimate concern about her daughter's friendship with a girl who believes she is homosexual. While we might as adults feel better if we could totally isolate our teens from any interaction with sexual promiscuity outside of marriage, that's not realistic in our world. Recognize that teens who want to talk about "friends" who are struggling with homosexuality may actually be trying to determine how you will respond to them if they are struggling with it. As you respond to teens' concerns about friends, realize you may actually be responding to their concerns about themselves. However for teens who have friends struggling with homosexuality, here are some ways to help.

- **Don't focus on sexuality.** If teens are going to have relationships with teens struggling with homosexuality, they need to keep the focus of the relationship on shared interests and activities, rather than letting the entire relationship focus on the homosexuality of the friend.
- **Set boundaries.** Help teens think about the boundaries of the relationship. The relationship needs to have clear boundaries about no physical contact. Similarly, there need to be boundaries about spending time exclusively alone.
- **Don't go there.** While teens can continue to interact with friends struggling with homosexuality, they shouldn't enter into the activities of the gay community. Teens who enter into the activities of the gay community will face pressure to change their views on homosexuality. Teens frequently do not have the decision-making and coping skills to handle this type of challenge to their faith.
- **Attraction alert.** Teens need to know if a friend who is homosexual is attracted to them. If the friend is sexually attracted to the teen, then it may be impossible for the teen to continue in a close friendship with the homosexual teen.
- **Don't try to "fix" it.** Teens aren't responsible for trying to "fix" friends who are struggling with homosexuality. Teens need to recognize they are responsible for their behavior, not their friend's behavior.
- **Know right from wrong.** If teens begin to seriously question biblical teachings about homosexuality, they may not be able to maintain their friendship with someone struggling with homosexuality. Teens need to be able to clearly articulate their beliefs and recognize that they can care about someone who is doing something wrong.
- **Ask for help.** Teens need to have adults they can talk to about their friendship and how it is affecting them. They need adults who will listen, be supportive, and hold them to biblical standards of conduct.
- **Let it go.** The most important lesson for teens is to learn to let it go,

so God can handle it. Encourage teens to pray for their friends struggling with sin. Help them see that God loves their friends more than they do and that he will hear their prayers.

■ **No way.** Despite teens' best efforts, there may be times they cannot maintain a friendship. If the friendship begins to focus exclusively on sexuality issues or if the friend is intent on drawing the teen into the gay lifestyle, the relationship will have to end. If a friendship ends, help teens recognize that they are setting healthy boundaries and making their relationship with God a priority.

I Can't Deal with This

If a teen tells us that he or she is homosexual, our immediate reaction is "I can't deal with this!" Talking about sexuality is difficult for most of us and talking about homosexuality will seem overwhelming to many of us. Yet we can, and must, be able to help our teens deal with their concerns that they may be homosexual. For us to be able to help teens who are struggling with concerns about homosexuality, the first thing we have to do is deal with our own emotional reactions to homosexuality.

Quite frankly, we live in a homophobic society. Being homophobic means that we fear homosexuality. From a Christian worldview, being homophobic means we fear people who are committing a sexual sin. A bit ironic isn't it? We don't fear people who are committing other kinds of sexual sins, but we fear people who are homosexual.

Yet because of this cultural homophobia, many of us have difficulties discussing homosexuality. If teens bring up homosexuality, we are immediately uptight and uncomfortable. If we are uncomfortable discussing the subject, teens will find other sources of information. When teens look elsewhere for information about homosexuality, they may actually go to individuals who will encourage them to pursue a homosexual lifestyle. Like all the other topics in this book, we want to be the ones having conversations with our teens because we bring a biblical perspective to the subject.

Why Can't I Deal with Homosexuality?

If you have a reaction of revulsion, hostility, or violence toward homosexuality, you need to examine why you feel this way.

■ You may have had previous negative experiences with homosexuality.

■ You may be influenced by our culture and the messages it sends about homosexuality.

- You may have had a homosexual encounter in your history.
- You may have been sexually abused by someone of the same sex.
- You may have been taunted by peers who labeled you homosexual.
- You may think homosexuality is a bigger sin than all other sins.

If any of these statements are true for you, you need to address your own concerns about homosexuality before you will be effective in addressing the homosexual concerns of teens.

From a Christian perspective, we need to treat individuals struggling with homosexuality the same way we treat individuals struggling with other types of sin. God didn't create an entire separate protocol for how to treat homosexuals, although many times in our culture it seems that people do have a different protocol for how to treat homosexuals. In the New Testament, Jesus repeatedly interacted with sinners. In fact, one of the Pharisees' complaints about Jesus was he spent too much time with sinners. When Jesus interacted with sinners, he treated them with dignity and respect. When we interact with people who sin, we should likewise treat them with dignity and respect.

In teaching our teens to treat others with respect and dignity, we should set firm boundaries about how homosexuality is discussed in our youth groups. There should be no tolerance of gay jokes or insults. Teens should not be allowed to use derogatory terms to refer to individuals who are homosexual. If we have teens that are struggling with homosexuality or are being labeled homosexual in our youth groups, we need to make every effort to insure that they are being treated with compassion and respect. Similarly, we need to recognize that we may have teens in our youth groups who have friends who are homosexual.

Figure It Out

Eric, a youth minister, noticed that Joe had been hanging around after youth group the past few weeks. Now, Joe was the only teen left in the room.

"Eric, can I talk to you?"

"Sure Joe, what's going on?"

"Well … um … I need to talk to someone about some stuff. I know the Bible teaches that homosexuality is wrong, but what is someone supposed to do if he is homosexual?"

"They are supposed to do what people who are heterosexual do. They're not supposed to have sex outside of a marriage relationship."

"Even if they don't have sex with anyone, they are still gay, aren't they? Just being gay is wrong, isn't it?"

"Joe different people struggle with different sins. All of us are sinners. Someone who struggles with homosexuality is just like someone who struggles with having premarital sex. Joe, you're asking a lot of questions about homosexuality. Do you know someone who is struggling with homosexuality?"

"It's not someone I know. It's me."

The next few statements Eric makes to Joe will have a profound effect on how helpful he will be to Joe. Eric knows that just because teens tell you that they are homosexual, it doesn't always mean they are. Many teens who will say that they think they are homosexual are actually struggling with misinformation, labeling, or sexual identity formation.

When a teen tells you that he or she is struggling with homosexuality, it is imperative that you obtain more information before indirectly confirming for them that he or she is homosexual. If teens are struggling with previous sexual abuse or peers making fun of them because they aren't masculine enough, your acceptance of their stated homosexuality will confirm that they are homosexual.

Rather than indirectly confirming that teens struggling with sexual confusion are homosexual, we need to assess the situation and provide teens with accurate information. We need to ask teens why they believe they are homosexual. Teens may inaccurately believe they are homosexual for several reasons.

- **Sexual abuse.** Teens who have been sexually abused by an adult of the same sex may believe that they are homosexual. They believe that perpetrators were attracted to their homosexual tendencies or that an abuse experience will define their sexual orientation for the rest of their lives.
- **Gender role issues.** Males who enjoy typically female activities or females who enjoy typically male activities may believe that these interests define them as homosexual. Engaging in activities that are typical of the opposite sex is not related to whether a person is homosexual or heterosexual.
- **Name calling.** Teens who have been harassed by peers and called derogatory names suggesting they are homosexual, may believe that they are homosexual. These teens may believe that other people recognize that they are homosexual, even if they don't believe they are. Other people don't define sexual orientation for teens.

■ **Sexual experimentation.** Teens may have actually had some sexual contact with a peer of the same sex. While this is certainly wrong, incidents of sexual experimentation do not define someone's sexual orientation.

■ **Homosexual friends.** Teens who have friends that identify themselves as homosexual may believe they are homosexual, especially if they did not recognize that their friends were homosexual. Occasionally teens may have homosexual friends who try to come on to them.

■ **Homosexual advances.** Teens who have had someone who is homosexual try to come on to them may believe that they are homosexual. Having a person who is homosexual try to pick you up does not define your sexuality.

■ **Emotional vulnerability.** Teens who are experiencing a life crisis (death in the family, chronic illness in the family, parental divorce) may be emotionally vulnerable. When teens are emotionally vulnerable, they will seek emotional support where they find it. If that emotional support comes from someone who is the same sex or someone who is homosexual, they may identify themselves as homosexual.

■ **Exposure to pornography.** Teens who have been exposed to pornographic materials may have seen or heard things that have changed their perceptions about sexuality and members of the same sex or the opposite sex. If teens have been exposed to pornography, what they have seen in the pornography may be leading them to believe they are homosexual.

■ **Poor sense of identity.** Teens may not have a clear understanding of their personal identity and may be influenced by media, peers, or adults to believe that they will find more gratification in a homosexual relationship than in a heterosexual relationship.

Common Misperceptions

■ **You can tell someone is homosexual by how they dress.** How someone dresses does not indicate their sexual orientation, it indicates their taste in clothing and style.

■ **You can tell someone is homosexual by how they act.** If a female is interested in "tomboy" activities or a male is interested in typically feminine activities, it does not mean they are homosexual. These behaviors indicate a lack of conformity to cultural gender roles.

■ **If teens are confused about their sexual feelings, they are homosexual.** Confusion about sexual issues is a typical developmental stage for adolescents.

- **You are homosexual if members of the opposite sex don't show a sexual interest in you.** Members of the opposite sex not being interested in someone, could indicate other interpersonal problems or that the teen just hasn't met the right person yet.
- **If you look at the bodies of people of the same sex, you must be homosexual.** Teens are concerned about how their bodies are developing. Looking at the bodies of members of the same sex may be about trying to establish identity or trying to establish a standard for physical appearance. It isn't necessarily about homosexual attraction.
- **If you are attracted to someone of the same sex, it means you will only be happy if you engage in homosexual activities.** People who experience an attraction of the same sex have dealt with these feelings and established healthy sexual relationships with members of the opposite sex.

Knowing What to Do

- **Stay connected.** If teens are struggling with homosexuality, help them stay connected with godly people who will encourage them to make good choices. If teens disconnect from their church family, they will make connections in the homosexual community.
- **Provide affirmation.** Affirm the positive qualities of teens. Help them see that they are beloved children of God even if they struggle with homosexuality.
- **Open up communication.** If teens have talked to other people about their struggles with homosexuality, they may have found that other people aren't comfortable discussing their sexual issues. Teens need someone to talk to, so keep the lines of communication open.
- **Tune in.** Teens who are struggling with homosexuality may feel alienated and unwelcome at youth group activities. Try to stay tuned into what these teens are feeling and respond to their emotional needs.
- **Get help.** Teens who are struggling with homosexuality need more help than you are equipped to provide them. Help them find a counselor who can help them find a godly way to deal with their struggles. There are also several Christian-based support groups to help teens deal with sexual orientation issues.
- **Sin is sin.** Help teens recognize that everyone struggles with sin. Just because our society places a stigma on homosexuality doesn't mean God considers it an unforgivable sin.

- **Don't focus on sexuality.** Don't let all the interactions you have with teens focus on their struggles with homosexuality. Focus on their spiritual development and other interests. Don't let them make homosexuality the focus of all their activities.
- **Focus on Scripture.** Help teens study the Bible to determine whether homosexuality is right or wrong.
- **Recognize the risk.** Teens take a big risk in telling you about their struggle with homosexuality. Telling you about these struggles is an expression of deep trust.
- **Keep it confidential.** Don't tell anyone else about what the teen is sharing with you unless the teen consents to you telling someone. If you need to talk with someone about the situation, talk with another minister or church leader without identifying the teen.
- **Give hope.** Although a struggle with homosexuality can be difficult, many Christians have overcome their desire for homosexual relationships. Help teens recognize that they can deal with this struggle.

In Over Your Head

As you consider what to do to help teens deal with homosexuality, recognize that there will be situations when you need to refer teens for professional counseling services to help them deal with homosexuality. If the answer to any of the following questions is yes, then you may need to refer the teen to a professional counselor.

- Has the teen tried to stop the homosexual activity and has failed to quit?
- Is the teen getting more involved in the homosexual community?
- Is the teen in a committed homosexual relationship?
- Is the teen receiving significant support from adults for homosexual choices?
- Is the teen significantly depressed or suicidal?
- Is the teen engaging in self-mutilation?
- Is the teen withdrawing from the youth group and other peers?
- Is the teen engaging in delinquent behaviors?

The Challenge

Teens are faced with more depictions of homosexuality and more acceptance of homosexuality in the media and the culture. As a result, they are more likely to have friends struggling with homosexuality or to have a homosexual approach them about forming a relationship. In response to cultural changes, many churches have become more strident in their condemnation of homosexuality. Yet these same churches have not been equally adamant about other sexual sins. Frequently, teens view churches as hypocritical in their response to homosexuality. Teens quickly realize that homosexuality is set apart as "the big sin," while other sexual behavior outside marriage relationships is ignored or forgiven.

Teens struggle to see how their faith is relevant in dealing with their friends who are homosexual or with their own concerns about homosexuality. If teens are struggling with concerns about homosexuality, they don't view youth workers and churches as resources that can help them deal with their concerns. Rather, they see youth groups and churches in general as forbidden territory for them if they have concerns about homosexuality. If we are going to be effective in addressing concerns about homosexuality, teens must recognize that we care about them and all of their struggles, especially their struggles with homosexuality.

RESPONDING TO THE CHALLENGE

1. If teens in our youth groups have friends struggling with homosexuality, how can we help these teens?

_____

_____

_____

_____

2. What are some reasons why adults are uncomfortable addressing homosexual issues?

_____

_____

_____

_____

3. Teens may believe they are homosexual when they are struggling with other issues. What are some issues that might cause teens to believe they are homosexual?

_____

_____

_____

_____

4. What are some common misperceptions about homosexuality?

_____

_____

_____

_____

5. How can we help teens who are struggling with homosexuality?

_____

_____

_____

_____

If teens limit the definition
of sex to intercourse,
they have permission to engage
in anything except intercourse.
Intercourse is a culminating event.
Sex is a process.

SECTION FOUR
HANDLING CHURCH ISSUES

The *focus* of this section of the book is helping you understand the need for policies and procedures in youth groups to protect teens from sexual predators. Similarly, these same policies and procedures help protect youth workers from false allegations and reduce a church's liability. In addition to looking at screening and training youth workers, this section addresses working with parents of teens.

The *purpose* of this section is to help equip you to deal with church leaders, other youth workers, church members, and parents.

Chapter 11
Don't Let It Happen Here

Chapter 12
Setting the Limits

Chapter 13
Connecting with Parents

It shouldn't surprise us that
our teens are exposed to
pornography when there are
more hard-core pornography stores
than McDonald's restaurants
in the U.S.
Teens are impacted by the
big business of pornography.
Phone companies estimate that
minors make 70% of the
500,000 daily calls to
pornographic telephone lines.
Similarly, it is estimated that
70% of all pornographic magazines
and videos eventually
make their way to
the hands of children.

11
Don't Let It Happen Here

The phone rings.

Mike is preparing a lesson for his Sunday Bible study. He sighs in frustration and answers the phone.

"Mike, there's a police detective here who wants to visit with you."

"Okay, send him back."

Mike wonders to himself about why a detective is here to see him. He figures one of the kids in the youth group must be in trouble. As Mike gets up to open the door, he realizes that generally he talks to probation officers, not detectives, if someone in his youth group is in trouble.

Mike introduces himself to the detective and asks, "What can I do to help you?"

The detective takes out his notepad and flips through the pages before clearing his throat. The detective frowns slightly.

"I'm here to investigate a complaint that has been filed against John Gilmore. A fourteen-year-old male reported that Mr. Gilmore forced him to engage in a sexual act with him during a church retreat last weekend."

Mike sits in stunned disbelief. His breathing becomes difficult. When he had taken this youth ministry job seven years ago, he had just finished his training and didn't have a clue about what he was doing. He had been young and enthusiastic, but didn't have any idea how to put together a youth ministry program. John Gilmore, one of the church leaders, was actively involved in the youth ministry when Mike took the job. Mike had relied on John's advice to help him establish relationships with teens and their parents in the church.

Mike can't believe what he is hearing. John had worked with teens in the church for nearly twenty years. There's no way John is sexually involved with a fourteen-year-old male. Is there?

Certainly, none of us would want to face the situation Mike is facing. Yet the recent attention targeted toward the Catholic Church points out a startling reality. Inappropriate sexual behavior between adults and teens does occur in churches. As devastating as the information has been about repeated sexual abuse in the Catholic Church, research indicates that it may be more likely for a teen to be abused in a Protestant church than in a Catholic Church.[1] Sexual abuse in a church is certainly not just a Catholic problem, it is a concern for every church.

Why Are Churches At Risk?

- **Too trusting.** Churches tend to accept others and trust people. Generally churches are not suspicious of their own members or visitors. Other organizations that work with children and youth aren't as trusting anymore. Because of previous incidents of sexual abuse, youth organizations typically screen their employees and volunteers to try to prevent sexual predators from accessing children through their organization. As other youth organizations have become more rigorous in their application processes for employees and volunteers, sexual offenders have gravitated more toward churches.
- **Behind closed doors.** The structure of church activities frequently provides an open invitation to sexual offenders. In many churches, one person may direct youth activities and classes behind closed doors. In addition, there may be several youth activities or church activities running concurrently, which makes it more difficult to directly supervise teens and the adults who work with them. As a general rule, churches provide abundant opportunities for a child molester to have close unsupervised contact with teens.
- **Volunteers needed.** Since churches frequently have difficulty finding volunteers to teach classes and supervise youth activities, any willing person is welcomed with open arms. Most churches still do not screen employees or volunteers who work with youth. Relative newcomers to the church, who for all practical purposes are strangers, are embraced and put to work immediately with teens, without any investigation into their backgrounds.

- **No criticism allowed.** In trying to maintain active volunteer participation, church leaders and members are reluctant to criticize people
who are willing to volunteer. If questions or concerns arise about a
volunteer's conduct, the church leadership may ignore allegations
rather than questioning the volunteer's conduct, character, or motive.
- **It won't happen here.** Finally, churches basically believe that they are
immune to any kind of abuse. Unknowingly, church members buy
into the belief that a person with dangerous or evil intentions would-
n't prey upon a church because it is sacred. The naïve trust placed
upon the institution is exactly what attracts sexual offenders. Churches
basically trust that their leaders and members will act appropriately.
- **Not one of our own.** In addition, church members buy into the myth
that a person who appears to be an effective spiritual leader won't
engage in inappropriate sexual contact with teens. The reality is that
a sexual offender may have exceptional social skills that invite other
people to trust him. One of the reasons sexual offenders victimize
so many different people is because they don't seem like they would
hurt teens.

Profile of a Sexual Predator

Heather is an outgoing fourteen-year-old who has attended
your church her entire life. Her parents have been active in teaching children's classes and working with newcomers to the congregation. Frequently Heather's parents invite new members of
the church and church leaders to their home to help new members become involved in church ministry programs.

Heather's parents are concerned when Heather comes home
after a mission trip to Mexico and seems withdrawn and emotional. After a week of watching Heather cry over insignificant
events, Heather's mother insists that Heather talk with her.
Heather shocks her mother when she tells her that she has been
sexually assaulted on the mission trip.

Several different church members accompanied the teens on
their mission trip. Decide which of the following individuals is
most likely to have sexually assaulted Heather.

- Todd is a strikingly handsome man in his late twenties. He is a middle-
level manager with a great future in the corporation where he works.
He has been married to his wife for six years and they have two

young children. He has been involved teaching in the youth ministry program at your church since his college years. The teens in the church love him. He is outgoing and loves to listen to music and watch movies with the teens. Since his children are young, his wife did not accompany him on the mission trip.

- Gerald has been involved with the youth ministry program for nearly fifteen years. Since Gerald's wife died two years ago, he has become a close personal friend of Heather's family. With no children of his own, he welcomed the chance to be involved in the family's activities. For most of the years he has attended church, he has devoted himself to reaching difficult teenagers. He has used his own money to take some of the most troubled teenagers on backpacking trips and fishing expeditions. He seems to gravitate toward the teens no one else can reach and is able to establish relationships with them.

- Patty is a married mother of three adult children. She has taught at the Christian high school since her own children started school there. She has sponsored yearbook and newspaper activities for years. During the time she has worked with journalism activities at school, she has frequently developed mentoring relationships with several female students over the years.

- Jared is new to the church. He moved to your city to take a job just out of college. He seems to have struggled to find a group of friends in the church and he indicates that he doesn't get along with his family. He is already having trouble with his boss at work.

Who did you decide was most likely to have sexually assaulted Heather?

Consider the criteria you used to decide who was the most likely suspect. Perhaps you decided it couldn't be Patty because she is a female and a mother. Or maybe you decided it couldn't be Todd because he is married. You might have ruled out Gerald because he is a close friend of the family. Probably, the majority of you thought that Jared was the most likely person to have assaulted Heather because he is new and seems to have trouble forming relationships with people.

The sad truth is that any one of the four is a likely suspect in the sexual assault. Although we tend not to trust a stranger or newcomer as much as we trust friends, over eighty percent of the time, the victim knows the abuser.[2] Most abuse takes place in the context of a relationship. Frequently the sexual molester invests a great deal of effort into gaining the trust of the teenager, the teen's family, and the church family. We can't look at someone and think we will recognize that he or she is a sexual molester. Sexual offenders look just like our friends and neighbors. They are often married and have children. They may commit sexual acts with males or females. They come from every racial, ethnic, economic, and religious group.

Quite literally, sexual molesters may be ministers, Bible teachers, youth leaders, camp counselors, or mission team leaders. According to the *Church Law and Tax Report* in 1996, volunteers commit fifty percent of the sexual offenses in churches, while paid staff members commit thirty percent of the offenses, and other youth, or children commit twenty percent of the offenses.[3] Child molesters can be captivating leaders who are able to motivate troubled youth to participate in church activities. Child molesters aren't necessarily socially inept drifters that can be identified as posing a threat to children.

Benefits of a Safety Program

Since we cannot identify child molesters by their appearance, occupation, social status, or ethnicity, we have the daunting task of establishing safety programs to ensure that teens are protected. A well-designed safety program has several advantages.

■ The program will discourage sexual offenders and child molesters from trying to access teens in your church. If you are screening your ministers and volunteers and another church in town does not have a screening procedure, then most sexual offenders will drift toward the churches without screening procedures because it is easier to access victims in those churches.

■ The safety program will protect your ministers and volunteers from false allegations of abuse. If your youth program implements and enforces policies for screening and supervising workers, then workers will not be placed in a position where they are vulnerable to false allegations.

■ The safety program will help churches reduce the risk of liability. If a teen makes an allegation against a minister, volunteer or church member, the court system can hold the church responsible for negligent behavior. The church is liable for any abuse that occurs in it facilities or at its activities, regardless of denial by the alleged perpetrator.

Resistance to Establishing Safety Programs

Despite the benefits of establishing a safety program, making a commitment to developing and implementing the program can be a difficult process for a church. There are several reasons why implementing a safety program may be difficult.

1. Church members do not want to believe that there is any possibility that a child molester is in their midst. Admitting the possibility that a sexual predator could be working with youth in a church makes the world a scary place for parents and teens.
2. Church members don't want to question the actions of youth workers. Questioning the activities of another church member may be viewed as insulting.
3. Churches don't establish safety programs because members believe the status quo is sufficient.

Church Safety Program Components

The following are the core components of a safety program:
- Provide educational seminars for volunteers, parents, and teens about the risks of sexual abuse, risk factors for abuse, and strategies to protect youth.
- Implement an application and screening process for all youth workers.
- Establish and enforce supervision policies for all youth activities.
- Develop a response plan to use if a sexual allegation arises.
- Carry liability insurance that includes sexual abuse coverage.

Selecting a Screening Committee

The success of a screening process will be determined in large part by how the process is implemented. Selecting a committee of church leaders to serve as a screening committee will be an important component of implementing the safety program. This screening committee will review applications, perform reference checks, review criminal background checks, and conduct interviews with potential youth workers. The screening committee should be limited to five to seven members. When possible, the committee members should serve for two or three years on the committee with rotating assignments. However, in some smaller churches it may be difficult to find enough qualified members to serve on the screening committee on a rotating basis.

The members of the screening committee need to be well-respected and mature Christians. The single, most significant characteristic of committee members must be their ability to maintain complete confidentiality concerning the information they learn about church members. The committee members may learn of criminal histories or previous personal indiscretions of church members. Church members must believe that the selection committee will be discrete with the information they learn about life histories. In addition, individuals serving on the screening committee need to be able to work well as part of a team and be able to communicate effectively with diplomacy and deference. Committee members need to be good thinkers and problem solvers who have no conflict of interests concerning who serves as youth ministry workers. Having professional experience in law enforcement, social services, counseling, education, or human resources work would be an added benefit for committee members.

Prior to serving on the screening committee, individuals will need to be screened by the church leadership. The members of the screening committee will need to complete an application. The church leadership will then need to check references and have a criminal background check conducted on individuals who will serve on the committee. Finally, the church leadership will need to conduct interviews with all of the potential members of the screening committee.

General Guidelines for Screening Youth Workers

■ Church leaders should not allow newcomers to immediately begin working with youth activities. A waiting period of six months or more should be required to help discourage sexual offenders who are seeking immediate access to children.

■ Volunteers and paid staff members should be required to complete an application. The application should include: name, address, phone number, social security number, employment history for the past five years, church history for the past five years, volunteer experiences for the last five years, training and skills for working with teens, personal references, consent to verify information and to contact references, permission to conduct a criminal background check, and a waiver of any right to confidentiality and of any right to pursue damages against the church caused by the reference's responses.

■ The screening committee should review the application. When reviewing the application, the screening committee should be looking for discrepancies in the chronologies of church membership, employment, or volunteer participation. In addition, the committee should look for changes in marital status and for past civil or criminal court cases.

■ A criminal background check should be conducted. There are several companies that conduct criminal background checks, as well as local law enforcement agencies. Generally, these companies or agencies charge a fee for conducting criminal background checks, so it will be important for church leaders to investigate the financial costs of the available options.

■ Once the screening committee has reviewed the application and the criminal background check, they should conduct an interview with the potential youth worker. The following issues should be addressed in the interview process:
* What are your strengths in dealing with teens?
* What type of role would you like to have in the youth ministry program?
* How do you redirect inappropriate behavior when working with teens?
* What do you find frustrating in working with teens?
* How do you handle these frustrating behaviors?
* What types of physical contact are appropriate when interacting with teens?
* What behaviors would you define as child abuse?
* What do you think will be the hardest part of working in the youth ministry program?

If no areas of concerns are identified in the screening process, then the church member should be utilized in the youth ministry program for a probationary period of up to six months. If any serious concerns about the individual's conduct arise in the probationary period, then he or she should not continue to work in the youth ministry program.

What If Concerns Arise in the Screening Process?

In the process of screening volunteers and staff members who work with the youth ministry program, the screening committee must develop criteria for excluding individuals from serving in the youth ministry program. Any adult who has been convicted of or pled guilty to any charge of sexual abuse, physical abuse, or neglect of a child should not be allowed to work with the youth in any capacity. Similarly, adults who have been convicted of or pled guilty to any of the following charges should not be allowed to work in the youth ministry program: contributing to the delinquency of a minor, child pornography, sodomy, incest, sexual assault, physical assault of a minor, kidnapping, or murder.

Similarly, a church should be extremely reluctant to use an applicant who has been charged with child abuse or molestation, even if they haven't been convicted. If the screening committee is considering using a church member who has been accused of child abuse, the police and prosecuting attorney in the case should be contacted to get additional information about the case. If someone has been charged, but not convicted of, sexually molesting a teen or child, he may still pose a threat to youth. An allegation of sexual molestation can be true, but the case not be prosecuted for a number of reasons.

Questions may arise in the church about forgiving someone for a previous offense and allowing him to heal and be used in church ministries. Certainly, a sexual offender can be forgiven for previous acts, but forgiveness shouldn't be equated with access to youth. Individuals who have a history that prevents them from working with youth can be utilized in other church ministries and integrated into the church family. However, anyone who has struggled with abusing children is always at a higher risk to engage in inappropriate behavior and should be provided the safety of a church family who acknowledges this and sets boundaries to protect the sexual offender and the youth of the congregation.

Whether the information in the criminal background check is pertinent to working with youth or not, it should be handled as highly confidential information. The church leadership and screening committee should take precautions to insure that the information obtained in criminal background checks is distributed to no more than one or two people. Not even all the members of the screening committee or church leadership need to know about the criminal background checks. With clearly established criteria for eliminating individuals from helping with the youth ministry program, one or two individuals can examine the criminal background checks and determine whether or not an individual can be used as a youth worker. If any questions arise, the information found in a background check can be presented to the screening committee without revealing the identity of the church member.

Warning: Extra Caution

Due to the realities of the legal system, many insurance companies strongly encourage that a safety program use an application that asks if an individual has been sexually abused as a child. In some court cases, rulings have indicated that churches are negligent if they don't ask youth workers if they are survivors of sexual abuse. On a cautionary note, most individuals who have been abused as children do not become sexual offenders. Asking about a history of sexual abuse is certainly a sensitive issue that must be handled delicately by church leadership.

Having a history of sexual abuse should not prevent someone from working with youth. Rather, the church has a responsibility to provide a higher level of care to adult survivors of child abuse. The church can discharge this duty by having adult survivors of child abuse meet with a church leader before working with youth. In this meeting, the church leader must assess whether the adult survivor has been able to heal from the child abuse situation. If not, the church leader should make a referral to a counselor and assist the individual in accessing the resources needed to heal from the abusive situation. If the church leader is convinced that the adult survivor has good boundaries and has resolved issues related to the trauma of previous abuse, then there is no reason why the person cannot be used in a youth ministry program provided that there is no criminal history of child abuse.

Preparing Churches for Change

Implementing a safety program is definitely a big change for most churches. In order to make the transition as painless as possible, it is important that church leaders and ministers promote the change in advance and allow the changes to be implemented gradually. The following steps can be taken to help prepare the church for implementing a safety program.

1. Church leaders need to meet with parents, ministers, and volunteers in the youth ministry program. The initial meeting should emphasize educating parents and volunteers about the risks of sexual abuse in church settings and then introduce the idea of a safety program. After the initial meeting, parents and volunteers need to have several weeks to ask questions about the program.
2. Church leaders need to establish a committee to develop written policies for the safety program and to nominate church members to serve on the screening committee. The committee should be given approximately six weeks to complete their tasks.
3. Once the committee has developed the written policies for the safety program and nominated church members for the screening committee, church leaders need to review the written policies and make any changes they believe are necessary.
4. Church leaders need to present information to the entire church about the risk of child abuse in church settings and then present the

safety program to the entire church. Church members should be given two to three weeks to express concerns or ask questions about the program. Church leaders need to recognize that sometimes individuals who express the most concern about a safety program may be the same individuals that should be a concern for the church.

5. Church leaders need to review the recommendations for a screening committee and appoint members to serve on the committee. It will take several weeks for the church leaders to review the applications of committee members, conduct criminal background checks, and to interview each committee member. The committee members will need to undergo an orientation program to prepare them for the tasks of the committee.

6. Once the screening committee is prepared, then church leaders will need to conduct a series of orientation meetings with all potential youth ministry workers. During the orientation meetings, the presenter will explain the safety program, and participants will be given the option of filling out an application or choosing not to participate in the youth ministry program.

7. The screening committee will have to review all the applications and authorize an agency to conduct criminal background checks on all youth ministry workers. Depending on the size of the church and the number of youth ministry workers, just reviewing the applications and criminal background checks could take several months.

8. Conducting interviews with existing youth ministry workers may extend the initial screening process from six months to a year. Because the initial screening process of existing youth ministry workers can be an overwhelming task in larger churches, some churches have opted not to conduct interviews with current youth ministry workers who have worked in the program for a significant amount of time. However, choosing not to interview existing youth ministry workers opens up the possibility of additional liability if an incident of abuse occurs in the church. The church leadership will have to balance the need to protect teenagers from potential abuse with the logistics of screening a large number of volunteer workers.

Obviously, initiating a safety program is no small task. Church leaders and members should expect the process to take six months to two years depending upon the size of the church. However, the benefits of protecting youth members from being sexually abused, of protecting youth ministry workers from false allegations of abuse, and of protecting the church from civil and criminal charges far outweigh the difficulties of initiating a program.

Checklist for Implementing Safety Programs

Yes No

☐ ☐ Are we screening all church employees and volunteers who work with the youth of our church?

☐ ☐ Are we conducting a criminal background check on all church employees and volunteers who work with the youth of our church?

☐ ☐ Are we training all of our church employees and volunteers to carry out our policies to prevent sexual abuse?

☐ ☐ Are we training all of our church employees and volunteers to recognize the signs of sexual abuse?

☐ ☐ Do our church employees and volunteers understand state requirements for reporting suspected sexual abuse?

☐ ☐ Do our church employees and volunteers know our reporting procedures for a suspected incident of sexual abuse?[4]

The Challenge

Traditionally churches have been reluctant to recognize that sexual perpetrators may use youth group activities to victimize teens. As a result, sexual perpetrators have been able to access teens in church settings. The recent attention directed toward clergy abuse of teens and children has helped churches recognize their vulnerability. However, once churches recognize their vulnerability, they frequently don't know how to protect their teens.

Initiating safety programs will help protect our teens from sexual predators and will help protect youth workers from false allegations of sexual abuse. At the same time, a safety program can significantly lower a church's liability. Initially church leaders may be reluctant to begin a safety program because they fear church members will resist its implementation. The key to successfully implementing a safety program is educating church members about the benefits of the program. If church members are convinced that a safety program will help protect teens, without unnecessarily violating the privacy of church members, they will support the program.

RESPONDING TO THE CHALLENGE

1. Why are churches at risk for sexual predators trying to access teens?

_____

_____

_____

_____

2. Church members frequently believe that they will recognize sexual perpetrators. Why is it difficult for church members to identify sexual perpetrators?

_____

_____

_____

_____

3. What must churches do to establish safety programs to protect teens from sexual perpetrators?

_____

_____

_____

_____

4. What do churches need to do to screen youth workers?

_____

_____

_____

_____

5. How do church leaders prepare church members for establishing safety programs?

_____

_____

_____

_____

Volunteers commit 50 percent
of the sexual offenses in churches,
while paid staff members commit
30 percent of the offenses, and
other youth, or children commit
20 percent of the offenses.
Child molesters can be
captivating leaders who
are able to motivate
troubled youth to participate
in church activities.
Child molesters aren't necessarily
socially inept drifters
that can be identified as
posing a threat to children.

12

Setting the Limits

Rudy, a youth minister, sticks his head inside the door of the youth classroom. Three senior high girls draped in oversized, old shirts are giggling and painting the walls of the classroom. He smiles at their enthusiasm and then surveys their progress. Mandy had approached him about painting the room several weeks ago. Rudy had initially been reluctant to let the three teens paint the room, but now he is appreciative of how much better the room looks.

Rudy returns to his office and begins to make phone calls to recruit parents to help with a retreat in the fall. He immerses himself in planning the retreat. A little after six in the evening, one of the teens, Mandy, knocks on his office door. He glances up.

"Rudy, we finished painting the classroom. You want to come take a look?"

Rudy glances at the clock and replies, "Sure, but I've only got a few seconds before I need to get home for dinner."

Rudy follows Mandy down the hall to the classroom. As they walk down the hall, Mandy chatters about the day's work and how much fun she had. When they walk into the classroom, Rudy immediately notices that they are alone and Mandy is standing very close to him.

"Where did Sandy and Judy go?" Rudy asks as he steps away from Mandy.

"Oh, they had to get home for dinner, but my parents don't care if I'm a little late. I wanted you to see how great the room looks. Doesn't it look great?" asks Mandy as she tries to move closer to Rudy.

"It looks great. I can't wait for everyone to see it next

Sunday." Rudy replies as he walks toward the door. He suddenly feels uncomfortable being alone with Mandy in the classroom.

Rudy walks back toward the office hoping the church secretary will still be in her office. Rudy listens half-heartedly to Mandy's stream of chatter. When he realizes the church secretary has all ready gone home for the day, he decides not to stop at his office and continues to walk with Mandy toward the parking lot.

Nearly six weeks later, the church leaders ask Rudy to meet with them after a church service. When Rudy asks what the meeting is about, he doesn't get a response. When Rudy opens the door to the meeting, he recognizes that something is wrong. No one is making eye contact with him. One of the leaders gestures to a chair and Rudy sits down.

"We have some serious issues to discuss with you. Several of the teenagers have been talking to their parents lately. These teenagers are voicing concerns about your relationship with Mandy. Mandy has been telling the other teens that the two of you are involved in a romantic relationship. These kids have been telling their parents that you are sexually involved with Mandy."

The church leader continues to speak, but Rudy doesn't hear anything else that is said. He knows that he hasn't been "romantically involved" with Mandy. She is a confused kid who is looking for approval and acceptance. As he sits in the meeting, he thinks back over all the extra chores and assignments that Mandy had volunteered to do for the youth ministry program. Most of the extra assignments had involved spending some time alone with him, but nothing sexual had ever happened. Because of her behavior the day she helped paint the classroom, he hadn't been alone with her again. He recognizes that even though he hasn't done anything wrong, his career may be over.

In this scenario, Rudy finds himself accused of inappropriate behavior when he did nothing wrong. Rudy could have avoided this situation, if he had established policies for supervising youth and had put those policies in writing.

Write It Down

Youth ministry programs benefit in several ways from having written policies for safety programs. First, having a written policy outlines clearly for all staff members and volunteers the expectations for their behavior.

Second, a written policy takes the pressure off individuals in making decisions about supervision at events because the established policy dictates the parameters for supervision. Third, an effective written policy, enforced by church leaders, helps reduce a church's liability.

Written Policy for Safety Program

A written policy needs to include the following components:
- A description of the application and screening process for staff members and volunteers who work in the youth program (as outlined in the previous chapter).
- Specific policies about supervision of youth in church activities and the consequences for violating those policies (as outlined in this chapter).
- A definition of child sexual abuse (as outlined in this chapter).
- An outline of the state's reporting requirements for suspected sexual abuse.
- A plan for reporting suspected child abuse (as outlined in the chapter).

The written child safety plan may include additional components, but these are considered the minimum standards for an effective safety plan. Before implementing a written child safety plan, the church's leaders should review the plan with the church's attorney and insurance carrier.

Policies for Supervising Youth

In the introduction to this chapter, Rudy's dilemma illustrates the most fundamental guideline for working with youth—don't put yourself in situations where you are one-to-one with a teen in a private situation. If for some reason, you must meet with a teen one-on-one, meet him or her in a public place or in a room with an open door where someone else can see you. Even if the teen is a female and you are a female, you need to be where someone else can see you. An allegation of homosexual contact between an adult and an adolescent can be as devastating, or more devastating, than a heterosexual allegation.

Two adults need to be involved in supervising all youth activities. New volunteers should be paired with an experienced youth worker for the first six months they are working in the program. Supervision by two adults needs to be provided until every teenager is in the custody of their parents or legal guardians. If someone who is not a legal guardian is picking up a teen, then youth workers need a note from parents indicating that they can release the teen into someone else's custody.

To be considered one of the two adults supervising any activity, an individual needs to be at least 21 years of age and some churches expect their adult supervisors to be a minimum of five years older than the youth group members. Many youth ministry programs utilize college students as interns and volunteers in their programs. However, as a general rule, college students should not be considered as adult supervisors for youth group activities. College students are close in age to high school youth and don't necessarily have the life experience to always make good supervision decisions.

In addition, college students often view high school students with romantic interest. Youth workers dating teens should not be permitted under any circumstances. Youth workers who indicate that they are romantically interested in a teen should be reassigned to another ministry immediately. Even though a college volunteer may be close to the same age as a high school student, the church faces liability for the college student's actions in most states because the college student is legally an adult, while a high school student is a minor.

When transporting youth, two adults should ride in every vehicle. If youth workers are transporting teens, they need to have written permission to transport the teens. If youth workers have to stop a vehicle in a non-public area for any reason while transporting youth, they need to immediately report the situation to their immediate supervisor at church. In addition, they should document the events in writing, in case questions concerning the situation arise later. In an emergency situation, if one adult has to transport a teen without another adult present, they need to transport more than one teen. As a precautionary measure, the youth workers should have the teens sit in the back seat, while the youth worker drives the car. In addition, if the youth worker has a cell phone, he or she should call and check in with a church leader to insure someone else is aware of the situation.

Youth activities and classes need to be conducted in rooms with windows or the doors of the rooms need to be propped open. Church leaders, ministers, and parents should be able to walk by any class or activity and clearly see what is happening inside the room. Church leaders and ministers should be encouraged to regularly visit youth activities to encourage and support youth workers. Having an adult regularly monitor the halls and premises during youth activities will help prevent teens from wandering off by themselves and will help prevent unknown individuals from accessing the building.

Church leaders need to establish guidelines for acceptable and unacceptable physical contact between youth workers and teens. Obviously, we want our youth workers to exhibit loving attitudes toward our teens.

However, in exhibiting a loving attitude, we don't want to place teens in the position of being exposed to physical contact that makes them uncomfortable or provokes lustful thoughts. Youth workers should avoid any type of playful or amorous physical contact. For example, rather than youth workers hugging students in frontal hugs, they can give side hugs —providing nurturing physical contact without the opportunity for teens to as readily misinterpret the gesture as having sexual meaning.

Supervision for overnight activities and out-of-town activities must be carefully planned. The screening committee must clear all youth workers and adult chaperones before they accompany youth on any trip. Even parents should go through the screening process if they are accompanying the youth group on an overnight trip.

Adult leaders need to provide high profile supervision of youth on overnight trips. Youth need to know that they are expected to be in their rooms at curfew and that adults will know if they aren't in their assigned rooms. Periodically through the night, adult leaders need to check hallways and rooms to make sure that youth members are safe. When youth members share rooms, adult leaders should be careful to assign teens to share rooms with other teens approximately their age, unless siblings want to share a room. Adult leaders should avoid sharing rooms with teens, unless everyone is sleeping in an open area. Sleeping in the same room with a teen or teens creates the opportunity for allegations of inappropriate sexual contact.

These supervision policies are not intended to address all liability issues that a youth ministry program might encounter, but they are intended to provide information that is specific to liability of sexually inappropriate behavior. It is assumed that the church will obtain written parental consent for transporting teens and for teens to attend activities. Furthermore, it is assumed that the church will carry adequate insurance and will consult with an attorney in developing policies and procedures to reduce the liability.

Training Youth Workers

The church leadership should provide an initial orientation meeting for new youth workers and an annual orientation for all youth workers. During the annual orientation meeting, church leaders need to review the supervision policies for working with teens. In addition, an annual orientation meeting provides an opportunity to review the warning signs of sexual abuse, consequences of sexual abuse, and procedures for reporting suspected sexual abuse.

Youth workers need to understand that any type of sexual relationship with a minor can result in a felony conviction, imprisonment, and identification as a sexual offender. In addition, youth workers should be told that the church insurance policy is designed to protect the church as an entity, not necessarily individuals who work in youth programs. The church insurance policy may not provide youth workers with monetary support for a legal defense or a court judgment against them.

Types of Sexual Contact

All of the following behaviors are considered sexual contact:
■ Touching genitals or breasts
■ Having an adolescent touch an adult's genitals or breasts
■ Putting objects or body parts (fingers, tongue, or penis) inside the vagina, mouth or anus of a adolescent for sexual pleasure
■ Showing pornography to an adolescent
■ Exposing genitals to an adolescent
■ Photographing an adolescent in sexual poses
■ Encouraging a minor to watch or listen to sexual acts in person or on video
■ Watching an adolescent undress without the adolescent's knowledge[1]

When you train your youth workers, you need to present specific information about your state's laws in regards to reporting sexual abuse of a minor. Every state has a mandatory law requiring that suspected sexual abuse of a minor to be reported. Each state specifies what activities constitute sexual abuse of a minor. The state law also details who is legally responsible for reporting suspected cases of sexual abuse. Generally states require that sexual abuse of minor be reported to either law enforcement or a children's protection agency. The state law stipulates how long a person has to file the report. Most states require that a report be made within 24 to 48 hours of discovery. Many states allow an anonymous report, but if you choose to report anonymously, you need a witness who can verify you did report your suspicions. Generally, if you suspect sexual abuse and do not report it, you can be fined or sentenced to jail. On the other hand, most states provide protection from criminal or civil litigation if you make the report in good faith.

Recognizing the Warning Signs

Youth workers need to be trained to recognize the warning signs of a potentially inappropriate sexual relationship. Adults who perpetrate against teens generally follow certain behavioral patterns. Perpetrators may frequently violate established supervision policies. For example, a perpetrator will spend time one-to-one with a teen even when policy requires two adults be present. When confronted about the behavior, the perpetrator may be able to give compelling reasons for spending time alone with a teen. Occasionally, a unique situation or an emergency may arise and an adult may have to spend some time one-to-one with a teen. However, the adult should make every effort to be in a public place. When church leaders should become concerned is when a pattern of this behavior emerges. A sexual predator will repeatedly find opportunities to spend unsupervised one-to-one contact with teens. Regardless of how compelling an individual's arguments may be for spending time one-to-one with a teen, church leaders need to have zero tolerance for any individual who repeatedly violates established safety policies.

A second area of concern is when adult workers begin discussing their problems with teens. Frequently, by discussing marital relationships or other stressful situations with teens, a perpetrator places the teen in the emotional role of a peer. By creating an emotional peer relationship with teens, the perpetrator begins to erase the boundaries established between adults and youth. Initially developing an emotional peer relationship with an adult can be flattering for teens. Eventually, the perpetrator draws the teen into a complex emotional relationship that overwhelms the teen's ability to cope. Once the teen is confused and overwhelmed by the emotional demands of the relationship, then the perpetrator initiates the sexual contact.

Sexual perpetrators may also show an unusual amount of interest in teens' dating and relationships with peers. Perpetrators may want to know the intimate details of the physical and sexual contact that teens are experiencing in their relationships with peers. In addition, perpetrators may show an unusual amount of interest in the sexual content in movies or music that are part of the teen culture. Typically, perpetrators use these discussions to desensitize the teens to sexual content and issues. As the teens become more desensitized to sexual issues, the perpetrator begins to initiate physical contact. The initial physical contact will probably not have any sexual connotation. Gradually, the perpetrator will move from physical contact to sexual contact. The initial sexual contact may be holding hands or kissing teens quickly, but gradually the sexual perpetrator escalates the behavior to fondling. Eventually the behavior will move from fondling to intercourse or anal penetration. Sexual perpetrators set their victims up carefully and gradually introduce sexual contact.

Responding to Inappropriate Non-Sexual Behavior

If youth workers suspect inappropriate sexual behavior, they need to immediately report their concerns to church leaders. In turn, church leaders need to immediately investigate and confront inappropriate behavior. If the inappropriate behavior involves spending time one-to-one with a teen without engaging in any physical contact, the church leadership should reiterate the safety program and have the worker sign a statement of warning. The statement of warning must describe the inappropriate behavior, state applicable portions of the safety policy, and clearly state that the youth worker will be removed from the youth ministry program if another infraction occurs. Church leaders need to closely supervise and monitor the youth worker for an extended period of time.

If the situation involves physical contact not overtly or intentionally sexual, then church leaders need to assess whether the youth worker should continue to work with teens. Church leaders have the option of having the youth worker sign a statement of warning or of completely removing the youth worker from the youth ministry program. If church leaders decide to remove the adult worker from the youth ministry program, then the worker should be restricted from participating in children's or youth ministries.

Responding to Allegations of Abuse

If a youth worker is accused of sexual contact as previously defined in this chapter, then the church leaders need to respond to allegations of sexual abuse. Anytime there is an allegation of sexual abuse, the first and primary concern should be the safety of the teen. If the allegation involves a current situation, then the teen must be removed from the alleged perpetrator's presence. Then the teen's parents and the church leadership need to be notified. Once a church leader is on the premises, he or she should notify the church's attorney, insurance agent, and the appropriate law enforcement or child protective services. If a church leader cannot immediately be on premises, then the youth worker should contact the appropriate law enforcement agency or child protective services. The church leader would still be responsible for notifying the church's attorney and insurance agent.

The church leaders should not confront the alleged abuser at this time. While it is certainly biblical to confront the alleged abuser, the church leadership should allow the local law enforcement agency to conduct an investigation of the situation rather than assuming the alleged abuser is guilty. Church leaders should immediately remove the alleged abuser from having any contact with the church youth. However, the church leaders should not respond with anger or hostility, but rather with kindness and respect. Remember, the alleged abuser may not be guilty. Don't jump to conclusions.

In case the church eventually faces litigation of any kind, it is imperative that church leaders and the youth workers initially involved in the situation carefully document every step that was taken by the church in response to the allegation. Be sure that the teen is kept safe and treated with compassion. However, do not let parents of the teen persuade you not to notify the appropriate law enforcement agency or child protective services. Parents may frequently believe that minimizing the number of people who know about the alleged abuse will be helpful to their teens. You must recognize that you need to comply with state law for reporting alleged abuse, and you need to cooperate with the ongoing investigation.

At the same time, take as many precautions as possible to protect the anonymity of the teen. Drawing extra attention to the alleged abuse or allowing it to become the gossip subject for other teens is certainly not a constructive approach. In many states, the identity of the teen can be withheld throughout legal proceedings. Church leaders may have to decide how much information they will share with the congregation. Although church leaders do not want to be deceptive in dealing with their congregation, they also need to be aware of the ramifications of their actions on the victim. Church leaders will be forced to balance the need of the victim for privacy and the need of the congregation for information. If the case attracts a great deal of media attention, obviously church leaders will need to address the issue with the congregation and be prepared to deal with questions from the media. When the church leadership addresses the congregation, they should make a brief statement to the church without giving any unnecessary details and without violating the victim's privacy.

The Challenge

A critical aspect of implementing a safety program is training youth workers to provide appropriate supervision of youth activities. If a church develops written policies for supervising youth group activities emphasizing the two-adult rule and accountability for adult interactions with teens, youth workers will clearly understand the expectations of the church leadership.

If youth workers have attended an orientation meeting and have a copy of the written policies for supervising youth activities, church leaders should expect compliance with the policies. If youth workers are not following the established policies for supervision, church leaders need to remove these workers from interacting with teens to prevent any potential harm to teens.

RESPONDING TO THE CHALLENGE

1. Churches need to develop written policies outlining expectations for youth workers. What should a written policy contain?

_____

_____

_____

2. What are some general guidelines for supervising youth activities?

_____

_____

_____

3. What must be covered in an orientation meeting for all youth workers?

_____

_____

_____

4. What are the warning signs that a youth worker may be interested in a sexual relationship with a teen?

_____

_____

_____

5. If a youth worker is ignoring a church's policies for supervising youth group activities, what can church leaders do?

_____

_____

_____

6. If a teen makes an allegation of sexual abuse, how must church leaders respond?

_____

_____

_____

13

Connecting with Parents

Gary fidgets as he waits in the hallway. The church leaders are meeting to discuss his leadership of the youth ministry program. This is his first job as a youth minister and he feels like he has done everything wrong. He loves working with the teens, but the parents don't seem to like anything he has done. He's tried to be innovative and relevant in his lessons in Bible class. He has changed up some of the established activities of the youth group and the teens seem to like the changes. None of the parents were happy about his changes.

A group of parents came to talk with him several months ago. The parents had voiced concerns about his lack of communication and how he seemed to disregard their input concerning events. Gary acknowledges to himself that the parents were probably right about ignoring their input. When he had taken the job eighteen months ago, the parents seemed overly concerned about his youthfulness and lack of experience. He had decided to prove to them that he could handle the job without their condescending advice. In hindsight, he thought that had probably been a mistake.

The parents would have probably forgiven his other mistakes if he hadn't started a sex education program in the youth group. The parents had gone absolutely ballistic about discussing sex in the youth group. The parents accused him of talking too frankly about sex and about giving their kids ideas about sex. They had angrily cornered him after church on Sunday and told him that he was finished working with their kids. They threatened to take their kids to another church if the church leadership didn't fire him.

The church leaders had met with those parents most of the afternoon. The parents hadn't spoken to him when they left the meeting, but at least they hadn't yelled at him.

The door to the conference room swings open and one of the church leaders motions for Gary to come into the room. Gary enters the room and glances around the faces at the table. He doesn't see welcoming expressions on their faces.

The man at the head of the table clears his throat and begins, "Gary, I assume you are aware that several of the parents in this church are quite concerned with your behavior."

Gary swallows hard and says, "Yes, sir. I'm aware that some of the parents are upset with me, but if you'll just let me explain ..."

Gary is cut off mid-sentence as the church leader continues, "These parents say that you have initiated a sex education program in the youth group without discussing the program with them. Is that true?"

"I guess so, but ..."

The church leader holds up a hand indicating that Gary should stop.

"Is it also true that you initiated this sex education program without discussing it with us?"

Gary realizes he isn't going to be allowed to explain his side of the situation and answers, "Yes."

"The parents say that you are discussing oral sex, masturbation, pornography, and homosexuality in this sex education program. Is this true?"

"Yes."

"It is also rumored that you have told some of the teens that their parents rules for dating are too strict."

"I didn't actually say that, but I guess that's what I thought."

"Would it be fair to say that you have basically completely ignored what the parents in this church have to say about what their children will be taught about sex?"

"I didn't intentionally do that, but I can see how the parents might feel like that's what I've done."

"As a church leadership, we don't want our parents excluded from what their teens are taught in our programs. We find your behavior to be totally unacceptable."

Hopefully other youth ministers will not find themselves in the same situation as Gary. Dealing with sexual issues in a youth group is a sensitive subject. Youth ministers should not ignore sexual issues, but they need to integrate parents in the development of sex education programs and policies on handling sexual situations in the youth group.

Youth ministers need to help parents recognize the importance of communicating to teens that sex is a wonderful part of God's design for married couples. Furthermore, youth workers and parents need to acknowledge that parent conversations with their teens about sex are important and healthy. Almost one in four teens view "morals, values, and/or religious beliefs as major factors in their decision to have sex. Youth workers must recognize that parents are more influential than friends in making decisions concerning sex.[1]

Knowing the Limits

In working with parents, it is important for youth ministers to recognize the limits of their influence and expertise. Believe it or not, parents don't want a 23-year-old who has never raised teens telling them how to do their job as a parent. In order to have credibility in talking about parenting, you need to have some real life experience. Real life experience can be several years of working with teens and their parents or actual experience parenting teens yourself.

Developing relationships with parents can be difficult for youth workers. Youth workers must recognize that sometimes parents feel threatened by the influence youth workers have in their teens' lives. Teens can idolize youth workers and volunteers. When this occurs, youth workers can have a great deal of influence over teens. As a result, parents may not have as much influence. On the other hand, some parents intimidate youth workers, and youth workers may unconsciously exclude parents from activities or communication because they feel inadequate. Parents are allies in youth ministry programs, especially when dealing with sexual issues.

When the youth ministry program is going to present information to parents, consideration should be given to deciding who will talk with parents. Certainly the youth ministers need to be part of a team who talk with parents, but if youth ministers are young and inexperienced, they may need to allow someone else to take the lead in working with parents. Similarly, the youth minister may want to use a panel discussion or an open discussion format for addressing sexual issues with parents.

What Parents Should Expect

■ **Communication.** Parents expect youth ministers to communicate what they are teaching about sex. Discussing sex, in any context, is a sensitive situation. Parents should know what their youth ministers are teaching their teens about sex and should be aware of the sexual issues teens are encountering in their daily lives.

■ **Information.** Youth ministers need to provide information about the youth culture and specifically about sexual issues. Parents need access to resource materials to help them understand teen development, teen culture, and how to discuss sexual issues.

■ **Respect.** Parents expect youth ministers to respect their understanding of their teens. Parents know their teens better than youth ministers and love their teens more than youth ministers because they have been a part of their lives for years. Youth ministers must demonstrate a respect for the parents' commitment in their teens' lives.

■ **Support.** Parents expect youth ministers to support their established household rules and their disciplinary actions. Certainly youth workers may not always agree with a parental decision, but they should not express their disagreement to the teen. However, if youth workers have significant concerns about the appropriateness of parental actions, they should discuss the situation with church leaders.

■ **Professionalism.** Youth workers need to understand the current research concerning teen sexuality and the teen culture. In addition, youth workers have an obligation to understand laws regarding teens and sexual activities.

What Youth Ministry Can Do for Parents

■ **Empower parents.** Despite common misperceptions, teens are still more influenced by their parents than their peers when they are considering moral or ethical issues. Parents need to recognize that they may not have as much influence about the clothes their kids like as they do about how their teens will view sexuality as a spiritual and moral decision.

■ **Create a strong parent peer group.** Provide forums where parents can visit with one another about their teens. Discussions can focus on guidelines for dating, social activities, and chaperoning events. Help parents find common ground and establish some degree of uniformity in expectations about sexual behavior. If all the parents are saying the same thing, it's more difficult for teens to say, "But John's mom lets him...."

■ **Consult with parents.** Include parents in decisions about how sexuality will be addressed in the youth group and make parents aware of sexuality information that their kids encounter.

■ **Say what parents can't say.** Teens will listen to youth workers when they won't listen to parents. Some times we can be more direct in addressing sexual behavior than parents can be.

■ **Encourage teens to consult parents.** Teens tend to discount what parents say. As youth workers we can enhance parents' credibility by endorsing what parents say. We can even encourage teens to solicit their parents' advice on sexual matters.

■ **Minimize peer input.** Youth workers can help teens recognize that the information they get from teens may not be accurate about sexuality and that peers may encourage them to engage in sexual activities without considering spiritual implications.

■ **Teach about youth culture.** Generally, youth workers understand youth culture better than parents do. Youth workers can strengthen their collaboration with parents by sharing information about the youth culture and sexuality. Although a seminar about youth culture might be effective, developing a letter to send to parents on a regular basis that shares current information about sexuality and youth culture is another option.

What Parents Can Do to Encourage Abstinence

Although youth workers do influence teens, parents still play a crucial role in the decision teens make about sexuality. Youth workers can help parents recognize that they can be influential in helping their teens choose abstinence. Parents can encourage teens to be abstinent in the following ways:

■ **Provide supervision.** Parents who provide a high level of supervision in parenting their teens are less likely to have teens engaging in sexual behavior.[2,3] Teens first sexual experiences usually occur in their own homes or a friend's house.[4]

■ **Be supportive.** Teens with supportive families are less likely to engage in sexual behavior at a young age.[5]

■ **Talk about sex.** Parents who can openly communicate about sex, reduce the likelihood of their teens engaging in sexual behavior.[6]

■ **Raise the age for dating.** The older teens are when they begin dating, the less likely they are to engage in sexual behavior.[7]

- **Attend church.** Teens who attend church are less likely to engage in sexual behavior.[8]
- **Expect good grades.** Teens who make good grades in school are less likely to engage in sexual activities.[9,10]
- **Talk about going to college.** Adolescents interested in going to college or pursuing a career after high school are less likely to be sexually active.[11]

Warning: Red Flags

While integrating parents into decisions about addressing sexual issues is important in youth ministry, there are some boundaries that need to be established. Youth workers need parental support and input, but parents need to recognize the limitations of what they can offer to the youth ministry when addressing sexual issues.

When it comes to sexual issues, teens generally aren't willing to disclose information if their parents, or the parents of their friends, are present. Admittedly, there are some exceptions to this generalization. Occasionally, there are parents who have been actively involved in youth group activities for a long period of time that can effectively address sexual issues. When parents join youth group classes or activities just when sexual topics are being discussed, the participation of the teens will be stifled. Youth workers can meet with parents at another time and present the lessons to parents, rather than trying to integrate parents into the teen activities, unless the activities are intended for both parents and teens.

Confidentiality is another area of concern. Church leaders and youth workers need to meet with parents and discuss the limits of confidentiality. Teens should reasonably expect that most of their discussions with youth workers are confidential. Parents need to respect the confidentiality of the relationship between youth workers and teens. However, there are clearly instances when confidentiality cannot be kept.

Warning: No Confidentiality

Confidentiality cannot be kept when:
- A teen is being physically or sexually abused
- A teen might hurt himself
- A teen might hurt someone else
- A teen needs parental consent for medical treatment

There may be other instances when confidentiality cannot be kept, but church leaders, parents, and teens all need to know and understand the parameters of confidentiality. Parents shouldn't expect youth workers to tell them everything. Conversely, teens shouldn't expect everything they say to be confidential. An awareness of state laws regarding confidentiality with teens will help church leaders, youth workers, and parents establish guidelines for confidentiality.

The Challenge

In working with parents, youth workers need to acknowledge the critical role parents play in their teens' decisions about sexuality. Youth ministries should integrate input from parents into decisions about teaching sexuality and communicating about sexuality in informal settings. Parents want to feel included in the decisions that are being made about their teens.

Crucial to developing an alliance with parents is recognizing that parents need encouragement not advice. You have to work to establish a relationship with parents. Parents need to feel like they are part of what is going on.

RESPONDING TO THE CHALLENGE

1. What are some of the limitations youth workers have in dealing with parents?

_____

_____

_____

_____

2. What should parents expect from youth ministry workers?

_____

_____

_____

_____

3. What can youth ministry programs do to help parents?

_____

_____

_____

_____

4. What can parents do to encourage their teens to remain abstinent?

_____

_____

_____

_____

5. How much information should youth workers share with parents?

_____

_____

_____

_____

SECTION FIVE
JUMP IN!
THE WATER'S FINE

The *focus* of this section of the book is connecting the most salient points of the book into a few ideas that will help you work with teens.

The *purpose* of this section is to help you recognize the importance of teaching teens about God's plan for sex in a marital relationship. Just teaching teens to wait is not enough. We must teach them the benefits of not engaging in sex before marriage. This section of the book contains one chapter.

Chapter 14
Making the Wait Worthwhile

In the midst of teaching
teens about abstinence,
let's not forget to teach them
about sex in a marriage relationship.
Frequently, we focus so much
on telling teens "Don't do it,"
that we forget to say
how wonderful sex is as
part of a marital relationship.

14
Making the Wait Worthwhile

Four years have passed since David Gonzales began working to improve his skills in dealing with sexual issues in his youth group. David is occasionally heartbroken at the pain he sees teens endure because of poor decisions about sexual behavior. Yet, even in watching the pain, he acknowledges his gratitude that at least he is aware of what is happening in the lives of the teens in his youth group. David has worked through his own discomfort about discussing sexual issues and, as a result, frequently has opportunities to help teens make sexual choices based on biblical principles. While the teens in David's youth group continue to experience more sexual challenges than he faced as a teen, they feel like they can talk to David and other youth workers about their concerns and mistakes.

Today, David is waiting to meet with Paul. Paul is getting married in a couple of weeks and called yesterday to see if he could talk with David. David is concerned. When Paul was in high school, he struggled with pornography use. David had worked with Paul for several months to convince him that viewing pornography was wrong. Ultimately, Paul had decided to quit viewing pornography, but it had taken almost a year of gradual progress for Paul to completely quit viewing pornography.

In the process of holding Paul accountable for his pornography use, David had many conversations about sexual issues with Paul. They had discussed masturbation, pornography, abortion, sexually transmitted diseases, and other topics. In the midst of these ongoing discussions, David had noticed that all their discussions seemed to focus on the negative consequences of sex, rather than on the role of sex in marriage. Gradually, David began to focus more of the conversations on how God created everyone as a sexual person. David wanted Paul to realize that God saw sex in marriage as good. He wanted Paul to understand that a sexual relationship with a marriage partner created a special bond and union between two people.

While David waits for Paul in his office, he wonders why Paul was coming to see him. He feels a little apprehension and is concerned that Paul may be having some struggles with pornography use again or some difficulty maintaining sexual boundaries in his relationship with his fiancée, Becky. As David considers the possible reasons for Paul's visit, Paul appears in the doorway.

"Hey David! How are you?"

"I'm great Paul. How about you?"

"I'm doing okay. It's just a few weeks until the wedding, so things are a little hectic. Becky's a little stressed about all the last-minute details, so I'm keeping a low profile when she's dealing with the wedding stuff."

"Sounds like pretty typical last-minute wedding details. Seems like most of the couples I've known have the same kind of stuff happen. Are you having any second thoughts about the wedding?"

"Oh no! I love Becky more now than ever, even if she is getting stressed about some silly stuff. My relationship with Becky is really great. We both are committed to putting God in charge of our lives and to being spiritual encouragers for one another. Actually, I didn't come to talk to you about wedding jitters or anything like that. I came by to thank you."

"Thank me?"

"Yeah. You helped me deal with some difficult stuff when I was in high school. You held my feet to the fire about the porn and got me to quit. You'll never know how much help and encouragement you were. I'm grateful for that, but I'm more grateful for all the conversations we had about God's plan for sex. Lots of my friends don't understand the role of sex in a marriage and that God intended for sex to create a special relationship between a husband and a wife."

"I'm glad all those discussions helped out."

"The other thing, all those talks did is they made it much easier for Becky and me to talk about sexual boundaries in our relationship and about sex once we are married. I don't think we would have waited for our wedding night if you hadn't talked with me so much. Thanks for taking time for me."

David remains speechless. It's seldom he ever gets to hear that his interactions with a teen made a profound difference.

The Rest of the Story

In the midst of teaching teens about abstinence, let's not forget to teach them about sex in a marriage relationship. Frequently, we focus so much on telling teens "Don't do it," that we forget to say how wonderful sex is as part of a marital relationship. Teens who haven't heard healthy messages about sex in marriage may struggle with a sexual relationship with their spouses. If sex has been presented as being sinful and unholy to teens, when they get married they continue to feel shame when they engage in sexual acts with their spouse. Like one young adult told me, "Everyone has always told me 'don't.' Now I'm married and I still think 'don't.' Why didn't anybody ever say it was okay when I'm married?" While it is certainly important to teach abstinence, we must teach it in a way that also openly endorses sexual pleasure and fulfillment in a marriage.

At some point, we must present more than abstinence, we must teach teens about healthy marriage relationships and the role of sex in those relationships. When we tell teens to wait, we must tell them about what happens after the waiting. Sex creates a special bond between two people, an intimacy not shared by others. Sex is a form of communication in a marital relationship. In healthy relationships, sex becomes an unselfish act with both parties interested in the fulfillment of the other party. We can't forget the rest of the story—God created sex.

Rely On Relationships

While the strategies and techniques discussed in this book will strengthen your ability to help teens, nothing replaces having a good relationship with teens. Teens will share their lives with you when they know you care. Taking time to listen to teens and to learn about their struggles will help build trust. Teens need relationships where they know that an adult cares for them and is able to assist them in dealing with sexual issues. Sometimes teens just need someone to listen and clarify the situation for them. They may need someone to talk with them about healthy dating relationships and good sexual boundaries. Occasionally, they need help dealing with pornography, homosexuality, sexual violence, or pregnancy. Regardless of what teens need to help them make good decisions about sexual issues, they always need an adult who will listen to them and care about what happens in their lives. The relationship is more important than strategies or techniques.

Your Greatest Resource

Although I hope and pray that the material presented in this book helps you learn to help teens deal more effectively with sexual issues, I want to point you back to God as your greatest resource in helping teens. While the techniques in this book might help open up communication about sexual issues, there is nothing more powerful than your spending time on your knees praying for the teens in your youth group. Our teens need us to be prayer warriors on their behalf. Likewise, your teens will benefit from your spending time in studying your Bible. The Bible teaches much more about caring for the souls of teens than anything I could write in a book.

The Challenge

The ultimate challenge in dealing with sexual issues with teens is to present accurate information that is relevant to them, while at the same time conveying that sex in marriage is God given. We have to teach teens ways to remain abstinent before marriage, while at the same time teaching them that sexual activity in marriage is pleasurable and fulfilling. Too frequently we have emphasized the importance of abstinence before marriage without emphasizing the importance of sex in marriage. While we are telling teens to wait until they are married, we also need to tell them why waiting will be beneficial when they are married.

Similarly, we can't get so consumed with strategies and techniques for discussing sex that we forget that having trustworthy relationships with teens is the cornerstone of dealing with sexual issues. Being available with accurate information and concern is more important than what we specifically say. Finally, praying for our teens is one of the greatest gifts we can give them. Knowing that we are on our knees on their behalf teaches them the power of God while expressing our concern for them.

RESPONDING TO THE CHALLENGE

1. In talking about sexual issues with teens, what do we typically emphasize? How much time do we spend talking about sex in a marriage relationship?

_____

_____

_____

_____

2. What can we do to make ourselves available for developing relationships with teens in our youth groups?

_____

_____

_____

_____

3. How does our own personal Bible study benefit teens in the youth group?

_____

_____

_____

_____

4. When we are praying for our teens, what can we ask God to do in their lives?

_____

_____

_____

_____

Finally, praying for our teens
is one of the greatest gifts
we can give them.
Knowing that we are on our knees
on their behalf teaches
them the power of God while
expressing our concern for them.

References

Chapter 1
1. Adapted from Bradley, L.J., Jarchow, E., and Robinson, B. (1998). *All about sex: The school counselor's guide to handling tough adolescent problems.* Thousand Oaks, CA: Corwin Press.
2. George Barna is the president of the Barna Research Group, Ltd., a marketing research firm located in Ventura, California. Barna has written more than two dozen books about ministry, the culture, and church dynamics. Barna's research is available on the Web at www.barna.org.

Chapter 2
1. Padgham, J.J., & Blyth, D.A. (1991). "Dating during adolescence." In R.M. Lerner, A.C. Petersen, & J. Brooks-Gunn (Eds.), *Encyclopedia of Adolescence* (pp. 196-198). New York: Garland.
2. Coles, R. & Stokes, G. (1985). *Sex and the American Teenager.* New York: Harper & Row.
3. Centers for Disease Control and Prevention (CDCP). (1999). 1996 *Youth Risk Behavior Surveillance System (YRBSS).* Available at: www.cdc.gov/nccdphp/dash/yrbs/suse.htm.
4. Santrock, J.W. (1990). *Adolescence.* 4th Ed. Dubuque, IA: William C. Brown, 28-29.
5. Fields, J. & Casper, L.M. (2001). *Current population reports: America's families and living arrangements.* Available at: www.census.gov/prod/2001pubs/p20-537.pdf
6. Dusek, J.B. (1996). *Adolescent development and behavior.* Englewood Cliffs, NJ: Prentice Hall.
7. Brooks-Gunn, J. & Warren, M.P. (1988). The psychological significance of secondary sexual characteristics in nine- to eleven-year-old girls. *Child Development, 59* (4), 1061-1069.
8. Flannery, D.J., Rowe, D.C., & Gulley, B.L. (1993). Impact of pubertal status, timing, and age on adolescent sexual experience and delinquency. *Journal of Adolescent Research*, 8 (1), 21-40.
9. Ibid.
10. Elkind, D. (1984). *All grown up and no place to go.* Reading, MA: Addison-Wesley.
11. Adapted from Bradley, L.J., Jarchow, E., and Robinson, B. (1998). *All about sex: The school counselor's guide to handling tough adolescent problems.* Thousand Oaks, CA: Corwin Press.

Chapter 3
1. Personal correspondence from John Delony.

Chapter 4

1. *Huge ratings for 'Friends' finale: Sitcom's 'Baby Episode' delivers record numbers for season.* http://www.msnbc.com/news/754450.asp.
2. Hepburn, M. (1997). A Medium's Effects Under Scrutiny, *Social Education*, 9, 246.
3. Schultze, Q.J. (1992). *Redeeming Television*. Downers Grove, IL: InterVarsity Press. p. 46.
4. Elizabeth F. Brown and William R. Hendee (1989). Adolescents and Their Music: Insights into the Health of Adolescents. *Journal of the American Medical Association*, 262, no. 12, 1659-63.
5. Christenson, P.G. & Donald F. Roberts, D.F. (1998). *It's Not Only Rock & Roll: Popular Music in the Lives of Adolescents*. Cresskill, NJ: Hampton Press, Inc. 36ff.

Chapter 5

1. Henderson, Jeffrey M. *Teaching Abstinence*. Brochure. U.T.-Houston Medical School.
2. Ibid.
3. Ibid.
4. Ibid.
5. Personal correspondence from Carole Carroll.

Chapter 6

1. Largent, Steve (2000). *Congressional Record*. Daily Edition, 146 (80), (June 22, 2000).
2. Statistics available at: www.enough.org.
3. Schlösser, E. (1997). The business of pornography. *US News and World Report*, vol 122, no. 5, p 42-50.
4. Ibid.
5. *Facts About Pornography*. Available at: www.helpandhope.org/facts.shmtl.
6. Ibid.
7. Roper Starch Worldwide Inc. *The America Online/Roper Starch Youth Cyberstudy 1999*. Available at: http://corp.aol.com/press/roper.html. Accessed June 21, 2000.
8. Lehart, A., Rainie, L., Oliver, L. Fox, S., Horrigan, J., Spooner, T., & Carter, C. (2001). *Teenage life online: The rise of the instant-message generation and the Internet's impact on friendships and family relationships*. Available at: http://www.pewinter-net.org.
9. Largent, Steve (2000). *Congressional Record*. Daily Edition, 146 (80), (June 22, 2000).
10. Strasburger V.C, Donnerstein E. (1999). Children, adolescents, and the media: issues and solutions. *Pediatrics*. 103:129-139.
11. Log-on Data Corporation. *White Paper on Issues to Consider*. Anaheim, CA: Log-on Data Corp; 1996.
12. *Violent and sexually explicit Web sites hold 'surfers' hostage* [press release]. Minneapolis, MN: National Institute on Media and the Family; September 1, 1998.
13. Schlösser, E. (1997). The business of pornography. *US News and World Report*, vol 122, no. 5, p 42-50.
14. *Facts about Pornography*. Available at: www.helpandhope.org/facts.shmtl.
15. *Violent and sexually explicit Web sites hold 'surfers' hostage* [press release]. Minneapolis, MN: National Institute on Media and the Family; September 1, 1998
16. Zillman, D., & Bryant, J. (1988). Pornography's impact on sexual satisfaction. *Journal of Applied Social Psychology*, 4, 518-544.
17. Ibid.
18. Ibid.

19. Personal interviews with college students.

Chapter 7
1. Henderson, Jeffrey M. *Teaching Abstinence*. Brochure. U.T.-Houston Medical School.
2. Centers for Disease Control and Prevention (CDCP). (1999). *1996 Youth Risk Behavior Surveillance System (YRBSS)*. Available at: www.cdc.gov/nccdphp/dash/yrbs/suse.htm.
3. Boyer, D. and Fine, D. (1992). Sexual abuse as a factor in adolescent pregnancy and child maltreatment. *Family Planning Perspectives*, January.
4. Centers for Disease Control and Prevention (CDCP). (1999). 1996 *Youth Risk Behavior Surveillance System (YRBSS)*. Available at: www.cdc.gov/nccdphp/dash/yrbs/suse.htm.

Chapter 8
1. Advocates for Youth. (1994). *Health Futures in Jeopardy: Young People and Violence*. Washington, DC: Advocates for Youth.
2. Warshaw, Robin. *I Never Called It Rape*.
3. Ibid.
4. The Alan Guttmacher Institute. (1994). *Sex and America's Teenagers*. New York, NY: The Alan Guttmacher Institute.
5. Miller B.C, Monson B.H, Norton M.C. (1995). The effects of forced sexual intercourse on white female adolescents. *Child Abuse & Neglect*. 19:1289-1301.
6. Gardner, M. (1994). Community: A Hidden fact of life for teens: Dating violence. *The Christian Science Monitor*, 86 (152), p. 12.
7. Sandmaier, M. (1989). Health Express: News: Battered Girlfriends. *Mademoiselle*, 95 (6), p. 104.
8. Yee, Amy (1999). Learning K-12: Gender studies for teens: Please leave your stereotypes at the door. *The Christian Science Monitor*, 91 (154), p. 15.
9. Roscoe, B., Strouse, J., Goodwin, M. (1994). Sexual Harassment: Early Adolescents' Self-Reports of Experiences and Acceptance. *Adolescence*, pp. 515-522.

Chapter 9
1. 1995 Gallup Organization study, quoted in the *Cincinnati Enquirer* 7 December 1995.
2. Hopper, Jim (1997). Child Abuse: Statistics, Research and Resources.
3. American Medical Association (1995). Sexual Assault in America.

Chapter 11
1. Clayton, M. (2002). Sex abuse spans spectrum of churches. *The Christian Science Monitor*, April 5. Available online at www.csmonitor.com/2002/0405/p01s01-ussc.htm.
2. Hammar, R.R., Klipowicz, S.W., & Cobble, J.F. Jr. (1993). *Reducing the risk of child sexual in your church: A complete and practical guidebook for prevention and risk reduction*. Matthews, NC: Christian Ministry Resources.
3. Cagney, Mary. (1997). Sexual abuse in churches not limited to clergy. *Christianity Today* v. 41 (October 6) p. 90.
4. Adapted from Hammar, *et al.*, *Reducing the risk of child sexual abuse*.

Chapter 13
1. *Warning Signs About Child Sexual Abuse*. Available at: www.stopitnow.com/warnings.htm.

Chapter 14
1. Survey by National Campaign to Prevent Teen Pregnancy. Available at: http://www.teenpregnancy.org/keepprrl.html
2. Biglan, A., Metzler, C.W., Wirt, R., Ary, D., Noell, J., Ochs, L., French, C., & Hood, D. (1990). Social and behavioral factors associated with high-risk sexual behavior among adolescents. *Journal of Behavioral Medicine*, 13, 245-261.
3. Walter, H.J., Vaughn, R.D., & Cohall, A.T. (1990). Psychosocial influences on acquired immunodeficiency syndrome: Risk behaviors among high school students. *Pediatrics*, 88, 846-852.
4. de Gaston, J.F., Jensen, L., & Weed, S. (1995). A closer look at adolescent sexual activity. *Journal of Youth and Adolescence*, 24, 465-479.
5. Moore, K.A., Miller, B.C., Morrison, D.R., & Glei, D.A. (1995). Adolescent sex, contraception, and childbearing: A review of recent research. Washington, DC: Child Trends, Inc.
6. Holtzman, D., & Robinson, R. (1995). Parent and peer communication effects on AIDS-related behavior among U.S. high school students. *Family Planning Perspectives*, 27, 235-240.
7. Moore, K.A., Miller, B.C., Morrison, D.R., & Glei, D.A. (1995). Adolescent sex, contraception, and childbearing: A review of recent research. Washington, DC: Child Trends, Inc.
8. Ibid.
9. Ibid.
10. Ostrov, E., Offer, D., Howard, K., Kaufman, B., & Meyer, H. (1987). Adolescent sexual behavior. *Medical Aspects of Human Sexuality*, 19:5), 28-36.
11. Kirby, D. & Coyle, K. (1997). Youth development programs. *Children and Youth Services Review*, 19, 437-454.

About the Author

Dr. Beth Robinson is currently a Professor of Psychology and Chair of the Department of Behavioral Sciences at Lubbock Christian University in Texas. She has worked with teenagers for sixteen years in a variety roles. She has been a junior and high school teacher, a foster parent, a camp counselor and teacher, a volunteer in youth ministry programs, a Bible school teacher and a counselor.

In addition to working directly with teens, she has helped prepare professionals to work with teens. She has taught counselors and school administrators in graduate classes at Texas Tech University; social workers, youth ministers, and teachers in undergraduate classes at Lubbock Christian University; and ministers in graduate classes at Lubbock Christian University.

Dr. Robinson is a licensed professional counselor, an approved supervisor for licensed professional counselors, and a certified school counselor. Since 1992, Dr. Robinson has worked in a variety of counseling positions. She is currently employed by the Children's Home of Lubbock, and has previously worked as a counselor for Panhandle Assessment Center in Amarillo, Texas; and Director of Counseling Ministries for Monterey Church of Christ in Lubbock, Texas.

She has written numerous articles for publication in *Counseling and Values, Journal of Multicultural Counseling and Development, International Journal for the Advancement of Counseling, The Journal of Humanistic Education and Development, The Journal of Theology and Psychology, and 21st Century Christian Magazine*. Along with L.J. Bradley and E. Jarchow, she authored the book by Corwin Press, *All about Sex: The School Counselor's Guide to Handling Tough Adolescent Problems*.

Dr. Robinson is in constant demand as a speaker and trainer in universities and churches across the country. In addition, she frequently serves as a consultant to congregations on issues related to counseling and working with teens and children in churches. She has been active in both church ministry involvement and community service.